HR FOR IMPACT

TESTIMONIALS

To increase value of HR requires a chorus of outstanding voices. Add Ilona's inspiring voice to this choir! In this book, she offers practical, experience-based, and useful ideas that will enable any HR professional. Her recommendations for committing to the business, delivering with integrity, and taking action and accountability will help realize HR's impact.

DAVE ULRICH, Rensis Likert Professor at Ross School of Business, University of Michigan and Partner at The RBL Group

Being more human is so important. At Xero we have a value called #human, which is about recognising our collective humanity at work. We take this very seriously. This is so needful in today's workplace and can drive so much value for people and business. Ilona, in her book *HR for Impact*, has provided valuable insights and perspective on why putting the 'human' back into 'human resources' is so important. I have had the pleasure of working with Ilona and have always found her direct, pragmatic approach to HR and people matters refreshingly effective. This is a must-read for all leaders, and especially for HR leaders who are looking to make a real difference in their business and drive value.

DAVID THODEY AO

Like any function, HR must be able to demonstrate why the issues it addresses matter to the business, what they should care about and why. *HR for Impact* masterfully articulates a view on the people issues most pertinent to emerging HR leaders by providing practical tips, tools and insights on how best to respond to the *how*, *what* and *why*.

As a distinguished and highly respected HR executive over many years, Ilona Charles has drawn on a vast reservoir of expertise, knowledge, and wisdom to produce a practical and powerful guide for HR practitioners looking to add value and contribute to the success of their business in an environment of perpetual disruption.

I highly recommend *HR for Impact* to all HR leaders not just because I've had the great privilege to work alongside Ilona and to appreciate, first-hand, the value of her counsel, but because the concepts and advice in this wonderful book will ensure the new HR leader has the answers to their questions and is oriented in the right direction long after putting the book down.

DOROTHY HISGROVE, National Managing Partner, People & Inclusion at KPMG

I had the good fortune to work closely with Ilona at Aconex. She was an incredible strategic partner and trusted advisor to me in my role as CEO. Ilona takes HR well beyond simple people management, with an approach that is highly strategic and is coupled with clear, direct and understanding engagement with leaders throughout the company. She had enormous impact on the performance of Aconex through her work developing our executive team and leading our talent management programs.

LEIGH JASPER, Former CEO and co-founder at Aconex

An excellent guide for upcoming HR leaders (and existing HR leaders looking to refresh their approach) so you can stay focused on what matters, achieve outstanding outcomes and have an enterprise leadership impact. Ilona is an outstanding HR professional, business leader and mentor and so to have her share these pragmatic insights and experiences for others to learn from is a gift.

LINDA HIBBERD, Chief People Officer at PEXA

I have been working with Ilona and shilo. for over a year now. From my perspective as a former CPO, Ilona just gets it. She understood me, my requirements and what I was looking for in terms of the level of capability and skill. Our conversations are more than just check-ins, but rather about how I am going in my role as a CPO and how can she help me more generally with her advice and mentorship. Ilona's guidance has been extremely valuable and I have no doubt other HR leaders will gain significant value from her pragmatic and wise advice.

SNEZANA JANKULOVKSI, Chief People Officer at Cybercx

Published by Grammar Factory Publishing, an imprint of MacMillan Company Limited.

Grammar Factory Publishing
MacMillan Company Limited
25 Telegram Mews, 39th Floor, Suite 3906
Toronto, Ontario, Canada
M5V 3Z1

www.grammarfactory.com

Charles, Ilona
HR for Impact: Practical Steps for HR Leaders to Build Influence and Thrive / Ilona Charles.

Paperback ISBN 978-1-98973-740-8
eBook ISBN 978-1-98973-741-5

1. BUS030000 BUSINESS & ECONOMICS / Human Resources & Personnel Management. 2. BUS071000 BUSINESS & ECONOMICS / Leadership. 3. BUS012000 BUSINESS & ECONOMICS / Careers / General.

Production Credits
Cover design by Designerbility
Interior layout design by Dania Zafar
Book production and editorial services by Grammar Factory Publishing

Grammar Factory's Carbon Neutral Publishing Commitment
From January 1st, 2020 onwards, Grammar Factory Publishing is proud to be neutralizing the carbon footprint of all printed copies of its authors' books printed by or ordered directly through Grammar Factory or its affiliated companies through the purchase of Gold Standard-Certified International Offsets.

HR FOR IMPACT

Practical Steps for HR Leaders to Build
Influence and Thrive

ILONA CHARLES

Contents

Introduction

In early 2019, I left my corporate career in Human Resources. I had only been in my role as Executive Director for three months. I was really enjoying working with the CEO, the work was interesting, and the organisation was a highly respected, iconic Australian institution. Yet I just knew in my heart that something wasn't right (I'm betting you can relate).

Not one to act rashly, although my partner may disagree, I took the Christmas break to think it through. Maybe I was just tired – it had been a full-on year, leaving a place I loved due to an acquisition and jumping straight into a new role. Arguably the largest role I had ever had. I was also travelling – a lot! Primarily to Sydney and Canberra, but it was almost weekly and when I wasn't travelling, I was writing, reviewing and reading a significant number of papers for the monthly executive team meeting and the board meetings. My kids, who are adults now (and were then), started asking me whether I would ever be home. This came as a real shock to me; it was the first time they had ever asked me this, and I had been working in pretty high-stress corporate HR roles since they were born!

After twenty-five years in the Human Resources profession, I felt like I was still trying to prove something. To myself? To others?

Why is it that working in Human Resources leads to continually feeling the need to prove ourselves? Even when we're clearly very successful and competent!

I have no doubt the description of regular travel, copious amounts of papers to review and read, and the impact on your families sent shivers down your spine as an HR leader. Are you working extraordinary hours, often into the night, to get the work done? Do you feel there is no real recognition from anyone that what you are doing is not only necessary, but contributing to the overall success and effectiveness of your organisation?

So, what is going on here?

In my view, the problem is clear: The Human Resources profession as a whole has a credibility problem!

It is alternately viewed as the soft and fluffy function in the organisation or the hard-nosed, compliance function that doesn't care about people at all! One of my friends refers to HR as Human Remains! And his wife used to work in Human Resources.

Unfortunately, the perception of HR and what the function does or does not contribute is very poor.

While it is not fair that a whole profession is tarred with the same brush, this perception places enormous pressure on HR leaders to constantly strive to prove themselves, time and time again.

If your role is not respected, as an individual you must work twice as hard to have any influence over critical stakeholders and any meaningful impact on key business decisions.

The fact is, HR is important because people are important.

In a year when the world has been in turmoil due to the global pandemic, the pressure on Human Resources professionals to work even harder and longer has never been so great. We have had to significantly pivot our attention to issues such as remote working, mental health and wellbeing, loss of jobs and redundancies, furloughing of employees, and understanding government grants and new employment laws to deal with the significant upheaval for workforces and employees everywhere.

At the same time, there has been a continued expectation that all the 'normal' work needs to continue. This is not sustainable; it wasn't sustainable before the pandemic and it is not sustainable now.

Increasingly, businesses and CEOs are understanding what a good HR leader can bring to their organisation. They certainly understand the importance of people. Unfortunately, many have yet to experience what 'good HR' looks like. I have heard this feedback many times.

While 2020 was a tumultuous and exhausting year, there is an enormous opportunity for HR leaders to significantly shift the perception of the Human Resources function.

Good HR leadership is about leading with influence and impact without burning yourself out in the process.

During my career, I have seen the best and worst of HR. I have also seen the best and worst of CEOs, senior executives and employees.

There are many books, white papers and programs you can read and attend on the technical competencies required to be a good HR practitioner. This book is not about that. It is not your technical competence that will set you apart from others in the eyes of senior leaders and employees, nor will it assist with your ever burgeoning workload.

In this book, I will provide insight into the attributes and characteristics I believe are essential for HR leaders today. After all, we are human and we work with other humans! Hence, there are certain qualities and expectations that are unique and essential to being successful in our profession.

One of the first things I faced when commencing this book was that I couldn't identify a single nomenclature for our profession or the executives who lead these functions. It struck me that this was yet another symptom of the credibility problem our function faces. Right now, the 'people' function and its senior leaders are variously called Human Resources Directors, Chief People Officers, Heads of, General Managers, or Executive Directors of: People and Culture, People Experience and sometimes just People!

For simplicity, I have landed on Human Resources (HR) leaders. Regardless of your title or whether you are an HR leader or aspiring to this role, this book provides pragmatic advice to support you to be the best you can be. I discuss the importance of our function, and why we need HR leaders who have the respect of their CEO, their peers and their teams.

The stories I have used throughout are based in fact. However, some poetic licence has been taken to illustrate or amplify a point; no offence should be taken. Names have been changed or not used at all to protect people's privacy.

We will focus on the three critical elements required to lead with influence and create impact as a senior HR leader in your organisation.

This is very much about putting the 'human' back into Human Resources, gaining respect and building credibility.

No one told me how to be a good HR leader and I can count on one hand the number of role models I looked to for guidance or inspiration. I will share my practical approach to HR leadership and share my learnings based on personal feedback and experience.

I am going to share with you what no one else tells you in the hope that this makes your life as an HR leader not only bearable, but enjoyable.

Ready?

PART I:

WHY WE NEED TO BE MORE HUMAN

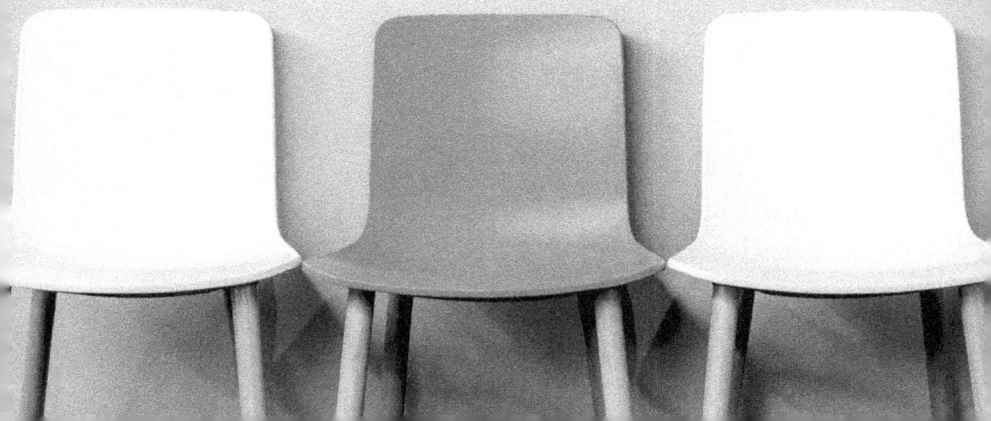

HUMAN RESOURCES HAS A PERCEPTION PROBLEM. THERE HAVE
been numerous TV shows depicting HR in a less than compli-
mentary light. Unfortunately, as we all know, perception is often
grounded in reality. HR and its various iterations over the last
thirty years, from the personnel function to people and culture to
people experience to talent, has a significant credibility problem,
not least due to the many name changes. The **human** in Human
Resources has been forgotten.

Yet we know that Human Resources is important. We know that
such factors as good leadership, employee engagement and feeling safe at work all lead to significant improvements in business
performance and productivity. Human Resources is the function
accountable for ensuring these occur. So, what has gone wrong?

Many HR leaders are still too caught up in day-to-day operations.
They are drawing on their technical expertise to solve complex
and challenging organisational problems that require more than
knowledge to solve. Significant focus on operational issues can lead
to senior HR leaders feeling overworked, undervalued and stressed.

HR leaders must evolve to a position of trusted advisor. This is
critical to an HR leader's success. It requires an ability to draw
on technical expertise at key points in time while focusing on
building strong and credible relationships with key stakeholders
in the business.

In the following chapters, we look at what has gone wrong in
HR and the evolution required to go from technical expert to
trusted advisor. We look at how to put the human back into
Human Resources.

Chapter 1

No Laughing Matter

We have all seen the portrayals of Human Resources managers on television and in the movies. Let's take a look at *Utopia*. *Utopia*, internationally titled *Dreamland*, is a Logie Award-winning Australian television comedy series by Working Dog Productions. It follows the working lives of a tight-knit team of bureaucrats.

Like all good comedies, the plot is based on aspects of real life. Beverley Sadler, played by Rebecca Massey, is the head of the Human Resources Department and an experienced recruiter whose main role is conducting exit interviews with staff members who have quit after three weeks in the job. She has strong views about performance management and has created complex and cumbersome processes, which she justifies based on evidence and research into the latest thinking and best practices. She also supports yoga in the office to lift morale and improve employee engagement.

The writers expertly take many standard Human Resources processes and turn them into something very funny. In series 2, the key characters, played by Rob Sitch and Celia Pacquola, are discussing an employee Celia believes needs to go. The scene goes something like this, starting with Rob Sitch.

'Pay her out.'
'No.'
'Can you promote her?'
'What? No.'
'Can you make her redundant?'
'Yes.'
'Without replacing her?'
'No.'
'Pay her out.'
'No.'
'You'll have to performance-manage her.'
'Okay.'
'That means involving HR ... [pause, Celia's face drops]... I said HR!'
'Pay her out!'

We sit and laugh nervously. It's very funny when it's on TV ... not so funny when you reflect and realise it's a bit close to the bone!

There are other examples. George Clooney plays Ryan Bingham in the film adaptation of *Up in the Air* – he works for a Human Resources consultancy firm specialising in termination assistance. He flies around the country firing people, while simultaneously building his frequent flyer miles and living the high life built on the misery of others. Or Drew Carey, in the *Drew Carey Show*, who was the Assistant Director of Personnel. Or Toby Flenderson, the HR Manager played by Paul Lieberstein in *The Office*.

I love these shows, but they all portray Human Resources in a rather unflattering and stereotypical way. HR sacks people and does not really care; HR creates complex processes and rules; HR is a bit boring and is very operational; HR is soft and fluffy; HR doesn't really understand what is important for our employees or the business. HR isn't really like this, is it?

Stereotypes should always be challenged; however, what these television and movie portrayals go right to the heart of is the credibility of the HR function in the eyes of colleagues, managers and employees. Perception is reality and the best comedy often reflects the realities of everyday life.

Human Resources is seen as a bit of a joke. The people who go into Human Resources are considered a bit 'out there' and are seen as either not caring about people or not understanding the businesses in which they work.

The irony of all of this is that the Human Resources function is seen as not very 'human'.

Human Resources is not respected as a profession and lacks credibility in the eyes of management and employees.

THE HR CREDIBILITY DEFICIT

This is no laughing matter and is hugely frustrating for HR leaders. I have a huge amount of respect for the many HR professionals I have worked with over my career; I count many of these people as my friends. However, the function needs to change.

Lucy Adams, in her book *HR Disrupted*, states that HR has lost its way and needs to find a new direction. I agree. If I hear the question: 'How do I get a seat at the table?' one more time, I will scream. What these HR leaders are really saying is: 'I haven't been able to influence my senior leaders on the people agenda and I am not considered worthy of sitting at the executive table.' Depending upon the personality of the individual asking this question, it may be stated with indignation or a sense that they have been unfairly left out, or with real frustration that their CEO or senior leader doesn't understand or see the value they bring every day, let alone how hard they are working. You may think this question has run its course; I can assure you, it is still being asked.

I recently attended a lunch for senior HR leaders; the majority were HR executives of very large Australian companies. The topic in focus was: 'Why aren't there more HR people on boards?' The conversation was exactly the same! I could feel my frustration building and I couldn't get a word in! I finally blurted out, much to the disgust of the previous head of a peak HR body, that HR's credibility has significantly deteriorated and that this is the key reason why HR people aren't on boards! I am not sure this was a very good idea from a networking perspective, but it certainly silenced the room!

The answer to this question is clear. The people making decisions regarding the composition of their board do not believe HR leaders have the right skills, expertise or business acumen to effectively contribute and govern an organisation.

*The real issue is that decision makers do not
believe an experienced HR leader can contribute
past what the decision maker already knows.*

This type of attitude is extremely disheartening for those of us who know this is not true. I am yet to meet an HR leader who is not focused on driving value for their business, so how has this happened? What erodes the value and the credibility of the function and how does this impact you?

THE PERCEPTION PROBLEM

Bringing the latest thinking and ideas to your work demonstrates your technical competence, innovation and problem solving abilities. Unfortunately, while best practices are good in theory, they are often not applied at the right time or with the needs of the business in mind. The TV shows and movies I described at the beginning of this chapter reflect this over and over again.

*If an HR initiative is not aligned or integrated with
the business strategy or there is no capacity to take
on another new initiative in the business, then it is a
waste of time and energy and erodes HR's credibility.*

Take performance management as an example. Not one manager I have ever spoken with thinks annual appraisals are a good use of their time or add any value to the company or the bottom line; it is a tick-box exercise to please HR. Many large corporates have now removed the annual appraisal as a result. In nearly all cases, this has translated publicly to 'we no longer do performance management'. So, we see a long list of HR professionals jumping to remove performance management. This is a very reactive approach, based on external ideas in other companies that may or may not have similar strategic objectives to your own. Do you see what I mean? This is not about whether performance management and appraisals are worthwhile or not; it is about your ability as an HR leader to determine what you need for your company and for your business, and what will drive sustainable business performance.

This point is also well illustrated in the blog 'HR Leaders as Trusted Business Advisors' by Charles H Green, who says in relation to employee retention programs: 'Rather than blindly pursuing employee retention programs, for example, have a point of view about the right level of turnover; about the payback, return on investment and pros and cons of alternative approaches to retention; and about the priority of retention among other general business initiatives. Clear general business thinking is the antidote to feeling one's expertise is unappreciated.'

Not only do these examples demonstrate a distinct lack of business understanding or a genuine focus on people, but the impact on you as an HR leader is significant. You will have worked extremely hard to implement these new initiatives, but you will feel your efforts have gone unnoticed or, potentially worse, been denounced and criticised as ineffective. Yet HR leaders continue to take this approach. As Albert Einstein said, 'The definition of insanity is doing the same thing over and over and expecting different results.'

*HR is not respected and, while attitudes
are changing, the prevailing perception
is that HR does not understand what the
business needs and does not add value.*

BUT HR IS IMPORTANT!

It is enormously frustrating as an HR leader to continually read
and hear that you don't add value or understand the business you
work for. You must be sick of it and wonder why on earth you
continue to persevere. But you do, and I have for over twenty-five
years. This is because HR is important! And never more so than now.

The year 2020 was one of turmoil, heartache, sadness and frustration for many. The impact the global pandemic has had on business,
the economy, mental health and wellbeing, and its impact on
the workforce and how people work, has been significant. The
silver lining is this has been the time for HR to take the driver's
seat and, hopefully, to shine. After all, in my experience, great
HR people perform exceptionally well in a crisis. But it has also
been an extremely stressful time for HR leaders. They have had
little time to think of themselves, as CEOs and executive teams
leaned on them to lead them and their teams through and out
of the crisis. Suddenly, the old views of HR disappeared into the
background as workplaces grappled with the impact of the pandemic on their employees.

It has taken a pandemic for many CEOs and employers to see

the value their HR leader can bring as they have navigated these challenges. COVID-19 has highlighted the importance of people and leadership. It should not have taken a pandemic to do so, but it has highlighted what HR has known all along.

_____

*If we support our people, support them
as individuals, engagement will improve
and productivity will increase!*

_____

As the immediate pressures of the pandemic start to ease, it will be important for HR leaders to capitalise on their new-found respect and visibility. CEOs and the organisations they lead need HR. Good people practices are critical to an organisation's successful delivery of its strategy and business objectives. Good CEOs understand this. They want and need good HR leaders; they desperately want an HR leader on their executive team who can help them lead their organisation.

Understanding the skillsets and mindsets required to support and enable your CEO and the executive team to be the best they can be is critical to your success and, more importantly, your advice and guidance will be valued and respected. The result of this is that you will have far greater impact. Your CEO will listen and act on your advice.

_____

*Feeling confident in the value you bring
to your organisation can bring a great
sense of relief and satisfaction.*

_____

But why is this so important now? In a year of unrelenting pressure, I suspect some of you are wondering why you do this role. I know it has taken its toll on you. But there is a huge opportunity here. This is the time to capitalise on the renewed focus on Human Resources, the benefits good HR and people practices can offer and the leadership you can bring to the whole organisation. But you cannot continue to do it in the same way you always have. It is not sustainable, and you will burn out.

Ultimately, working harder and longer hours to get the work done and to prove your worth (although you may not think this is what you are doing) will not only damage your health and your desire to continue in the role, but will also negatively impact your credibility as an HR leader. This is because you are potentially focusing on the wrong things.

If you feel stuck, overworked, undervalued and exhausted, then something needs to change.

BEING MORE HUMAN

We need to look at a new way of working. As the saying goes: 'What got you here won't get you there.' We know that organisations need great HR leaders, now more than ever. We continue to be frustrated by CEOs and management who don't value our work or understand what we are trying to achieve. Of course, it takes two to tango, but what can you do to drive the change we need in HR? Continuing to complain that we don't have a seat at the table or continuing in the same way we always have won't drive the change we need. It certainly won't make your role any easier or improve your credibility.

As an HR leader, you are an expert in your field. As a graduate, you will have learnt the foundational technical expertise you needed to do your job. As your career progressed, you may have decided to specialise. Well-known specialist disciplines include industrial or workplace relations, organisation design and development (OD), learning, leadership, talent, remuneration and benefits, health, safety, wellbeing (although this is not always considered Human Resources), technology and systems, data and analytics, change management, payroll, workforce planning ... the list goes on. You may have gone down the generalist path, become a business partner supporting part of a business (or a whole business in a smaller organisation) with their people strategy. For these roles, you need to have a broad understanding of all the specialist domains. Different organisations will structure their functions according to their needs and strategic focus. Whether these disciplines reside in the HR function or not does not really matter. They are all focused on people and either enabling or de-risking the organisation.

There is no set path to executive level roles within HR, although with most organisations strategically focusing on attracting and retaining the very best talent, many Human Resources Directors (HRDs) have significant organisational development experience. Many OD professionals are also organisational psychologists. This used to be the critical entry qualification into Human Resources functions. Not so much now.

As you move into more senior Human Resources roles, you need to understand the key principles, skillsets and mindsets of leadership.

There are many leadership books, courses and experts you can tap into for this (you of all people should know this and have access to these resources). However, there are some key differences for HR leaders. CEOs and other executives expect more than just good leadership from their HR Director. The CEOs I know and have worked with want someone they can talk to, someone who will not only coach them but support them to lead their teams. They want and need someone they can trust.

The move from technical expert to trusted advisor, fellow executive and business leader is a critical transition for the HR leader. You have a powerful and important role to play in driving the organisation's success.

To do this, you need to become less reliant on the theory and your technical expertise.

We need to take a pragmatic and practical approach to our craft, remembering that what we are doing is working with humans.

Real people, with real needs. We are, as Lucy Adams describes, 'human-being experts'.

GAINING RESPECT

Knowing and understanding the critical elements of good HR early in your career can set you up for great success. To a degree, we all perform work and activities that are not intrinsically enjoyable. Positive psychology describes 'flow' or 'being in the zone' as a mental state where you feel completely immersed in your activity, with an energised focus and enjoyment in what you are doing. Wouldn't it be wonderful to feel like this in your role? It is not impossible.

Competence can lead to improved self-confidence. If you understand what is important and why, this can go a long way to building your confidence. In my experience, those leaders who are confident in their own abilities, their direction, their focus and their interactions with critical stakeholders are the ones who are the least defensive, deliver what the business needs and somehow manage to have a life outside work!

By building your own sense of ease with yourself and what you should be focusing on, you will build credibility within your business. Your colleagues and CEO will respect both you and the function you lead because you are adding value to them personally and to the growth of their business. Michelle Sales, in her book *The Power of Real Confidence*, states that 'confidence is the expectation of a positive outcome'. She highlights that with consistent effort and with the courage to take a risk, we can gradually expand our confidence and our capability to build more of it.

The learnings I have gleaned in my roles over many years of trial and error, together with a sense of self-worth and confidence in who I am and what I can bring, has led to a successful career in

Human Resources. Most of this was learnt the hard way, with many periods of intense workload and stress.

I share my experiences in the hope that you can avoid some of the pitfalls along the way, while learning to take ownership and accountability for the role you play in determining the credibility of HR.

———————

Understanding what a CEO really needs from their HR leader and taking a practical and pragmatic approach to your role will earn you the respect you deserve.

———————

Unfortunately, there is no silver bullet. But wouldn't it be nice to feel like you have things under control? To reduce your stress levels and feel like a real person again; someone pleasant to be around both at home and at work. And feel like the work you do and the function you lead are valued and credible in the eyes of your CEO, management and all employees.

The Buddhists have a good piece of advice: 'Act always as if the future of the universe depended on what you did, while laughing at yourself for thinking that whatever you do makes any difference.'

You can laugh at yourself, but HR is no joke. After all, we have a powerful and important role to play in making our organisations a great place to work. A place where people feel safe, valued and recognised for the work they do, each and every day.

———————

People really do matter. So, let's put the 'human' back into Human Resources.

———————

PERCEPTION IS NOT ALWAYS REALITY

Over the last few years, the perception problem HR is facing has become abundantly clear to me.

When I joined Aconex as the Chief People Officer in 2016, I had come off a long stint in the corporate world. The culture of Aconex was refreshingly different and confrontingly honest. In my first month, there were two interactions that really made me think about the perception of my profession. The first was at my first 'all hands' staff meeting. I was standing up the back near the beer taps (yes, they had beer taps – it's a technology company!). Leigh Jasper, the CEO and co-founder, introduced me to the team. I had to wave to be seen and called out to say I was near the taps. 'Jokingly' Leigh made a comment about hoping I wouldn't have them removed. He didn't mean anything by it, but it was a direct swipe at my role in HR. I instantly felt defensive and countered that I liked a beer just like everyone else! I did subsequently go on to prove this with gusto.

The second interaction was when somebody asked if I'd heard about the Christmas Party. We were in July! I innocently said 'No, why?' They proceeded to tell me it was a dress-up event. 'Okay,' I said, 'I haven't been that big on dress-ups, but okay.' 'No,' they stressed, 'it's not just any dress-up event; everyone, and I mean everyone, must dress up.' 'Okay,' I responded, 'well, if everyone is doing it, I can do that.' I had this conversation with more than one person. Each time I responded the same way, and there was a palpable sense of relief on the other person's face. They would then go on to tell me the whole event was a pretty big celebration (read 'alcohol'). I think this was probably the underlying point they were trying to make. That is, it could get a bit messy and how would I respond to that? To this day, I'm still not sure why they desperately needed to tell me in my first few weeks about the Christmas Party. I can only surmise that it was because I was in HR and they had a perception that HR (or at least HR they didn't know) might shut the whole thing down.

It's these types of interactions that have led me to thinking about how wonderful it would be if HR wasn't seen as such a joke or as the thought police! I know the value HR can bring and we should not have to be constantly proving ourselves.

Chapter 2

From Technical Know-How to Credible Influence

SOMETIMES THE MOST ANNOYING AND FRUSTRATING THING about working in Human Resources, particularly as you move into HR leadership roles, is that you start to see some of the worst as well as the best of human behaviour.

A good friend and colleague of mine recently moved into her first senior HR leadership role. She was suddenly exposed to politics and posturing that she had not seen before; it wasn't pleasant. It was a step above anything she had previously had to deal with. Her immediate manager was behaving a bit strangely and a new CEO had recently started. It was no coincidence that these things happened simultaneously. Complicating matters, the new CEO wanted to roll out a restructure that would impact her manager. Suddenly, she found herself in the middle of mayhem! Smack bang in the middle! Where had it come from?

As HR leaders, we often have to deal with sensitive issues. This was swiftly the case for my friend. One of the senior women in the organisation made allegations of sexual harassment against the same manager, but did not want to make a formal complaint because she didn't want to make a 'fuss'.

The HR leader role is not easy. All of this fell to my friend to resolve – and quickly. Because of the uncertainty and fear swelling in the organisation due to the new CEO coming on board, her manager started to pressure her for information. He was a senior executive – he knew what was going on and what she would know. 'What do you know?' he demanded. 'You need to help me. You're in HR – you must know what's going on?' The manager my friend had previously thought was okay to work with was starting to look decidedly not okay. All of his insecurities were coming to the fore and putting her in a very difficult position. Now *she* started to feel harassed. Sound familiar?

Nothing you have read in a textbook will equip you to deal with a situation like this. All the technical expertise you have built up over many years will fall away as if you never learnt it in the first place. My friend is a highly competent and talented HR leader, but she had never felt so hopeless and helpless, and she doubted her ability to deal with any of it. The individual issues were not outside her abilities to deal with or address, but the politics, posturing and poor behaviours really impacted her confidence and her stamina. She wondered whether she should be doing the job at all.

While it has continued to be a challenging role for her, my friend has navigated the complexities of this particular situation and undoubtedly been successful in her role and in resolving this matter. It has, at times, taken a toll on her health and wellbeing, but she has built incredible resilience and determination and a better understanding of how, in her role, she can add value and impact to the organisation.

Dealing with politics and poor behaviours
is not uncommon for HR leaders.

But no amount of technical know-how will enable you to deal with the situation adequately.

KNOWLEDGE IS NOT ENOUGH

No one had told my friend how to be a good HR leader. No one had told her what to look out for when she got to this level. Observing others deal with these things is very different from the lived experience. Politics is just one aspect of the complexity and challenging circumstances HR leaders often find themselves in.

What I have found over my career is that no one really tells you what good looks like. You go through your career blindly pushing on, hoping you are doing the right thing. You may not have done an HR degree; HR professionals come from many walks of life and backgrounds. Sometimes, like me, you sort of fall into it. I started my career as an Occupational Therapist. And like any degree, an HR degree will only teach you so much. It will teach you the technical competencies you require to perform the job with some degree of knowledge and skill. No qualification really teaches you how to thrive in an organisational context.

I have been fortunate enough over my career to have some great role models. Not many, unfortunately, but enough. You may feel you haven't had any. There seems to be a dearth of good role models in HR leadership roles. Why is this? What is so unusual about HR that means there are limited role models to learn from?

_____

Can you recall a great HR leader who inspired you and role-modelled great leadership behaviours? What did you learn from them?

_____

What have you learnt from those who didn't?

Most people learn from watching others, seeing what behaviours are rewarded and who is promoted. We often assume that they must be doing the right things ... mustn't they? This theory is fundamentally flawed. Like the concept of merit, we all know that some people get promoted who are not particularly good at their job. This is no different in HR. They might be very good, though, at reading or playing the politics, building relationships, and influencing the right people at the right time. These are important skills for all leaders to understand, but how HR leaders utilise them and for what purpose is critical to their credibility.

Some of the issues and problems you face at the HR leadership level are not dissimilar to what you might face earlier in your career. But they will definitely be more complex and more stressful. Unfortunately, they can sometimes seriously impact your confidence, your reputation and your desire to move into further leadership roles. Your role as a senior leader in HR is very different from other roles and functions across the leadership team and your technical expertise is not enough to get you through.

There are nuances and expectations of an HR leader that are different from those that come with other roles, and rightly so.

What do I mean by this?

As an HR leader, you will be privy to information that others are not. This automatically puts you in a position of power and influence, whether you like it or not. Depending upon the culture of the organisation and the leadership, others may be suspicious of you, your role and what you will do with this information. Being aware of this fact is a good first step. But awareness is never enough. You will need to work hard to overcome biases and pre-conceived ideas of what HR does or does not do. Your knowledge and technical know-how enable you to provide information in a timely manner and solve tactical problems; they will not enable you to build quality relationships where individuals like those described earlier feel you provide a safe haven where hard issues can be discussed without judgement. People need to trust you. All employees, no matter their level in the organisation, need to feel, when they are with you, that at that point in time you care about them and are treating them as an individual (a human). They need to believe that whatever they are raising with you is important.

Your credibility as an HR leader is directly related to your ability to flex comfortably between your technical expertise and your relationship skills. Every employee needs to know you are reliable, that you act with integrity and that you are there to support them. This is the definition of a trusted advisor. Throughout my career, I count as my role models those leaders who have supported me without judgement, supported me to grow as an individual, listened when I have needed them and made me feel they truly care about me as a person. In many cases, the line between manager and friend became blurred.

Understanding how to drive value for your organisation by drawing on your technical know-how and relationship skills at the right time and in the right way places you in a powerful position.

Technical know-how alone is not sufficient.

HR FOR IMPACT

Nearly every white paper, article or book I have read that discusses the transformation of Human Resources focuses on the function itself. Organisations have been transforming Human Resources for more than twenty years and yet, according to Bersin by Deloitte ('High-Impact HR: Building Organisational Performance from the Ground Up', July 2014), forty-two per cent of global companies report the impact of HR operations on organisational success is 'weak' and eighty-five per cent of global companies believe they must 'transform HR to meet new business priorities'.

The article demonstrates that when HR operates with impact, businesses out-perform. There is no one I have ever spoken with who would not agree with this statement. Figure 2.1, taken from the same article, shows that companies that implement HR models with impact 'are far more able to adapt to market changes, accelerate introduction of new products or services, operate efficiently and win over the competition'. Bersin and Deloitte are referring to their trademarked 'High-Impact HR Model'; however, the principles hold true for any HR model designed with the same intent.

Figure 2.1: Effects of a high-impact HR model

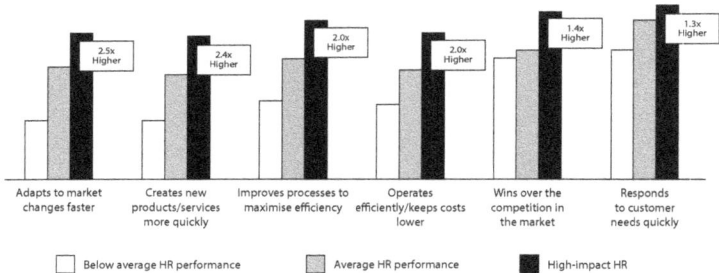

Source: *High-Impact HR: Building Organizational Performance from the Ground Up*, Bersin by Deloitte, July 2014.

So why do businesses still not value HR? And how come you, as an HR leader, continue to work harder and longer with seemingly little progress, credibility, influence or recognition?

The answer is because little has been documented regarding what makes a good HR leader. Think about HR organisations you have worked in and perhaps are leading now. How much time is spent on technical 'stuff' versus coaching, mentoring and relationship building?

I bet you are really busy. All the time?! So busy that you don't have time to do the things you want to do. So busy putting out fires, solving problems, juggling life and dealing with difficult people that you don't have the time or inclination to focus on what is really important as an HR leader – building trusted relationships with your most critical stakeholders.

FIVE MISTAKES HR PROFESSIONALS MAKE

HR functions are renowned for making simple processes complex.

Complexity drives busyness.

HR leaders who only draw on their technical expertise and know-how create complex processes and solutions to technical problems. Consequently, a lot of time and effort is put into implementing complex solutions that often don't add substantial value for anyone.

According to David Maister, author of *The Trusted Advisor*, there are five mistakes HR professionals make:

1. They overemphasise the technical
2. They don't listen
3. They jump quickly to action – keen to deliver results

4. They focus on the answers

5. They focus on me, not we

I am not suggesting for a minute that there shouldn't be the appropriate policies and procedures in place. This is a core requirement of any HR function's responsibilities; however, a credible HR leader will view processes, methodologies, frameworks and techniques as a means to an end. If they are useful and they work, then great – but if not, they discard them. The key test must be the question: Will this be useful for our employees and our organisation?

The other challenge with focusing too much time and energy on technical solutions is that you will be seen and described as 'too operational' and 'not strategic enough'. How often have you heard this? You have probably said this yourself about members of your team or other leaders across your organisation. The irony is that you are probably thinking, 'I don't have time to be strategic! I am too busy dealing with all the technical stuff that comes my way!'

Busyness has other consequences. If people around you see you as always busy, they are unlikely to seek you out on the things that really matter. Many times in my career I have had team members say to me, 'I didn't want to bother you with this – I know how busy you are.' On the surface, this seems quite lovely and very understanding; however, every time this happened it caused me significant concern. If this was how my team perceived me, how was I presenting to everyone else? My peers, my CEO? Were people coming to me with the things that were really important or were they avoiding me? Was my ability to influence and impact critical organisational outcomes being diluted because I was inaccessible and too busy?

Knowing how to flex between being a technical expert and a trusted advisor is the difference between being busy and inaccessible and leading with influence and impact.

CREDIBLE INFLUENCE

As you gain more experience as an HR leader, you will be required to deftly move between being an expert in your field and being a mentor, advisor and coach. Good CEOs and senior leaders understand the importance of HR. Reliability, integrity, empathy and discretion are the most important characteristics for an HR leader's credibility. In the diagram below, I have illustrated the progression from technical know-how to trusted advisor. This is the critical difference between being seen simply as an expert in your field and an HR leader who has credible influence, as shown in Figure 2.2.

Figure 2.2: From technical expert to trusted advisor

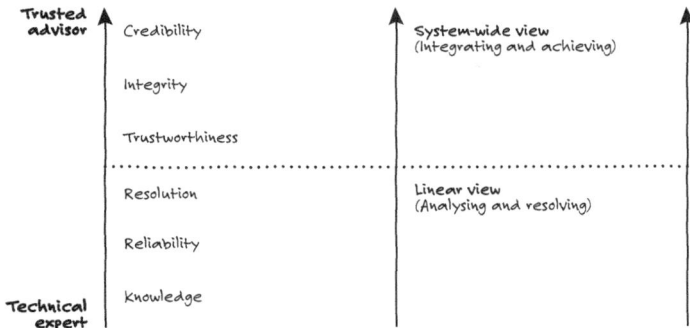

Let's look at each of these stages in more detail.

Knowledge: Your depth of expertise in subject matter related to Human Resources. Your understanding of the facts, information and skills required to do your job, gained either through education, experience or both. Hopefully, the theoretical and practical application of this knowledge. This typically includes: employee relations (basic employment law); performance management; the basics of remuneration, reward and recognition; talent management, including employee engagement. You may have done a more specialised undergraduate degree in organisational psychology, occupational health and safety, or business.

Reliability: The degree to which you produce stable and consistent results. You are applying your HR expertise, knowledge and advice consistently. People can rely on you to deliver and do what you say you are going to do. The critical element here is consistency. If you apply your knowledge in one way with a particular issue, for example, an employee issue related to performance management, then it is important to apply this advice consistently with your different stakeholders. This does not mean your advice cannot evolve, but you need to build a reputation for reliability first. Without this, your advice will be questioned, analysed, debated and challenged, which will lead to you feeling deflated and stressed. However, I am not naïve enough to suggest this may not occur anyway. Some managers or employees will never like your advice, no matter how reliable you are!

Resolution: This is problem solving. Using your skills, knowledge and experience to solve problems for your business. Problem solving is a critical competency for HR professionals. You are dealing with people and complex issues involving humans, and all that comes with human behaviour. Here you are starting to add real value to your business and stakeholders. You are tasked with defining the problem, understanding the variables, looking at alternatives, and evaluating and selecting those alternatives. It will require you to have a degree of creativity, plus analytical and research skills. To resolve a problem, you may also need to engage with other stakeholders. This will require you to confidently seek out other points of view to build your case. Your ability to resolve problems will be needed throughout your career. You will constantly need this skill as an HR leader.

Trustworthiness: Can you be trusted? This is about honesty and reliability. Combining the characteristics that have preceded it, trustworthiness requires you to have expert knowledge, be reliable and resolve issues for your business. Reputationally, you will hear comments such as: 'I can depend on her to get things done,' 'They always do what they say they are going to do,' 'They listen to my problem/issue and come back with consistent, but well thought through advice.' Once again, consistency is a critical characteristic. Sometimes, you will not get the resolution right. Everyone makes mistakes. Owning your mistakes or taking on board feedback, demonstrating a degree of humility and always being honest will help build your reputation as a trustworthy HR professional. Here, you are starting to take a system-wide approach, integrating your knowledge and experience to successfully work with people and resolve problems. To admit to mistakes can be scary, particularly in environments or cultures that do not support failure. This is where fear can start to undermine your trustworthiness; worrying about your credentials and how you are perceived can seriously start to undermine all the good work you have done.

Integrity: Building on trustworthiness, this is the quality of being honest and having strong principles. It also picks up elements of doing what you said you were going to do. This is about being ethical and showing consistent and uncompromising adherence to principles and values. CEOs expect their HR leader to demonstrate more of this characteristic than any other of their executive team. You may not think this is fair, but you are the executive who should be the custodian of the company values and you should be clear on your own personal values. It is your role to call out hypocrisy and challenge where appropriate. This takes courage. You need to be very clear on what is important to you and to the company in terms of behaviours. You need to hold a level of self-belief and stand true to your convictions. People will not always agree with you, but they will respect you for acting in accordance with the values, beliefs and principles you claim to hold.

Credibility: The sum of all the preceding elements of the model. To be a credible HR leader, you need to combine your expertise and experience with the critical traits of trustworthiness and integrity. The best and most respected HR leaders demonstrate all these qualities. Taking a system-wide view of your role, you are integrating information from many sources, including your own experience; you are clear on your values and what is important; you are confident in yourself and willing to take a stand when necessary. You are a role model for your team and your peers. You are enabling your organisation to get the very best out of its people.

To be credible, you need to not only understand Human Resources, but also the business in which you work.

THE BENEFITS OF BEING A CREDIBLE HR LEADER

One of the benefits of being a credible HR leader is that time can be spent with the most important decision makers in your organisation. Building a relationship with your CEO where you have credibility based on trust will free you from time spent on inconsequential projects and tedious day-to-day processes.

Your views will be sought by your peers, your CEO and your team on both personal and professional matters, and your opinions will be valued. An HR leader with credibility is sought for their wise counsel and understanding. Deploying the skills required to engage in these types of relationships is far more rewarding and enjoyable than developing a new policy or procedure or producing templates, documents and proposals. These relationships enable you to participate in debate and discussions where you may not agree with the other party, but there is constructive conflict and a mutual respect for each other and the outcomes you are trying to drive.

The most significant reward is that you can be yourself.

You are not using all your energy to protect yourself, defend your-self or justify your actions. You will feel comfortable with who you are and cease to feel hopeless and helpless.

This is not easy and it has taken me many years to feel confident enough to be myself in my role.

In Part II, we start to explore the critical attributes you will need to develop in order to move from being an HR expert to an HR leader.

A STEP IN THE RIGHT DIRECTION

Sally was a brilliant organisational development professional whom I had first met in a previous role. She was confident, assertive and smart. I was in my first HR Director role in a new organisation and I desperately needed people around me with the right skills and expertise to prove I could deliver what the business was asking. I wanted to lure her from a well-paying job in a large Australian corporate. Quite frankly, I never thought she would come and work for me or a smaller organisation, and I couldn't pay her what she was currently earning.

I had previously come across OD people who were a bit fluffy. The ones I had met never really understood the business. Sally was different. She was pragmatic, commercial and results focused, all attributes I respected and valued. Surprisingly, she accepted my offer and, true to her form, she delivered some exceptional results in a short space of time. After a few years, I decided to move on to greener pastures. I felt I had done everything I needed to do and needed a change. My CEO sought my views on whether we should look externally or whether I had the right talent in my team to step into the role. Sally was responsible for our succession planning across the organisation and she was fairly and squarely in my 'ready now' category (HR speak for she could quite capably do my job!). She knew this, given her role, and so I suggested she put herself forward.

Bizarrely, she wouldn't put her hand up for the job; she actively declined to participate as a potential candidate. She didn't think she could do it. She said she wasn't ready (yet she knew I had put her in the 'ready now' category). There didn't appear to be any rational reason for her not applying, except that she hadn't previously held a generalist HR role and hadn't followed the 'normal' HR career trajectory. This could only come down to her self-confidence – her belief that she wasn't up to it or couldn't do it. She was in a leadership role, but her responsibilities remained largely technical.

The company went external and spent months going through the normal talent search process. Finally, Sally put up her hand and expressed interest. And she got the job. She has been in the HRD role at the same organisation for many more years than I was, and has survived changes to CEOs and other significant organisational change. She had the skills, the mindset and the ability to do that role. While she didn't believe it at the time, Sally had built significant credibility and influence in the business in her previous role. She was able to apply her expertise where needed and build trusting relationships. She had learnt to flex between the linear approach to problem solving and a system-wide approach to relationships. She didn't do this consciously, but she did have a good role model!

PART II:

THREE STEPS TO CREDIBILITY AND INFLUENCE

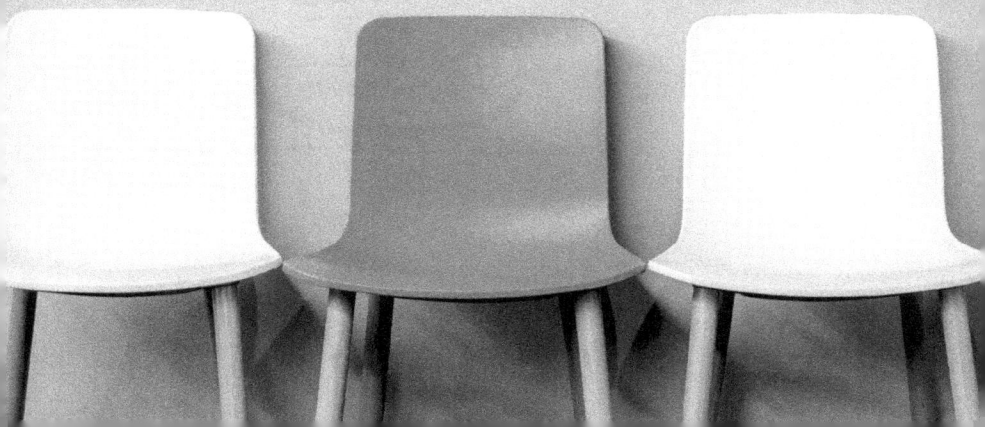

IN ORDER TO ACHIEVE YOUR CAREER ASPIRATIONS AND HIT THE ground running as an HR leader, you need key attributes, behaviours and knowledge that will enable you to influence business outcomes and strategy and have significant impact across your organisation. Your success as an HR leader is not defined by your technical know-how alone.

Most of these elements I have learnt through experience; none of these are found in HR textbooks.

As shown in Figure A, to build credible influence you need to:

1. Commit to the business,
2. Deliver with integrity, and
3. Take action and accountability.

Figure A: Three steps to credible influence

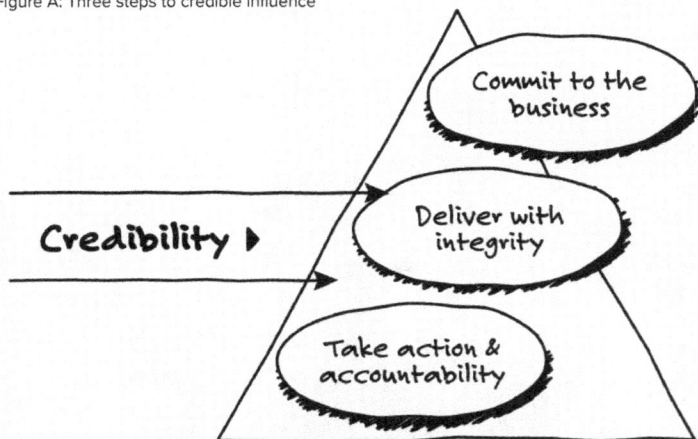

Commit to the business – As an HR leader, you need to understand and commit to the business in which you work. This requires HR leaders to demonstrate a level of commerciality and to understand the critical drivers of organisational success. 'Good' CEOs view their HR leaders as critical members of the executive team; this means taking accountability for business performance and delivery of the strategy. This part of the book explores what it means to commit to the business in which you work, demonstrating why it is so critical to you as an HR leader and how you might go about building this commitment.

Deliver with integrity – As a senior Human Resources leader, it is not only necessary but expected that integrity is core to who you are. CEOs expect their HR leaders to be role models, upholding the values of the organisation and the behaviours expected of the rest of the workforce. Delivering with integrity enables you to build trust and gain loyalty. This part of the book explores the relationship between trust and integrity and why this is more important for the HR leader than any other executive in the team.

Take action and accountability – HR is often described as reactive, overwhelmed and unresponsive. HR over-complicates and over-engineers solutions that do not deliver on critical business outcomes. The HR leader must take action and accountability for the services, solutions and initiatives the HR function delivers. The reality is, the pressure on HR leaders to perform is enormous and can lead to periods of significant stress and, in some cases, burnout. While there is no silver bullet, this part of the book focuses on four critical actions you can take to deliver pragmatic, useful HR solutions and free up some time for you to focus on what is most important to you, whether that be at work or at home!

In the following chapters, we will look at how you can get more impact from your approach to HR leadership through these three steps.

Chapter 3

Commit to the Business

In one of my earlier HR leadership roles, I knew I needed a fantastic talent acquisition lead to develop a compelling employee proposition and to support the company in its global growth aspirations. We needed the best people across the globe in a tight talent market. I had a particular person in mind, whom I knew from a previous role. He had an amazing reputation as a very talented HR professional. We met over a coffee and, as it turns out, he was as keen to work with me as I was with him. I broadened the role, so it provided him with scope, global oversight and the opportunity to really expand his own skills. A few months in, it was obvious to both of us that something wasn't right. The team loved him, he was doing some great work, but he just wasn't happy. It turns out he didn't like and didn't understand the type of business we were in.

When he joined the company, he spent most of his time internally with the HR team. He spent a lot of time understanding current HR practices, the processes, what was in place, what was not and a significant amount of time with his team members. Consequently, he built great working relationships with his team and those close to the team in other jurisdictions. He was a brilliant people leader. When it was clear he was not happy and not himself at all, we had a good chat and he was frank with me – he would probably leave to go back to an industry he loved. I was devastated, but not about to stand in his way.

Disappointingly, he had spent no real time trying to understand the business we were in. He spent very little time with the teams who built our product. I encouraged him to go and sit with the software developers who were super passionate about what they and the company were doing. He didn't. I encouraged him to spend time with other senior leaders to understand their work, how it contributed to the business, why it was important. He didn't. He read the company strategy, but did he have a grasp on how the SaaS revenue model worked and how it translated to company profitability? Probably not. He didn't understand SaaS, but he also had no interest in trying to understand it. He had made his mind up that this industry wasn't for him, yet had taken no real time to try to understand it. If he had tried, he may have come to the same conclusion, but I would have been okay with that because it would have been an informed decision.

The bigger issue for me was that there was no real desire or commitment to understand the business we were in.

He is a wonderful person, and a great friend – dedicated, talented and results focused, but without a commitment to understanding how the business works, it is very difficult to build credibility in the eyes of senior stakeholders.

UNDERSTAND YOUR BUSINESS

What the story above illustrates is that to build credibility as an HR leader within your organisation and with critical stakeholders, including your CEO, your peers outside the HR function, and your own team, you need to understand and commit to the business in which you work.

Gaining credibility requires commitment to learning, and a genuine curiosity about the business in which you work.

HR is, unfortunately, not seen as very commercial at all. In a recent article by Nick Holley, 'What CEOs want from HR', one of the senior leaders interviewed stated:

> *HR has its own drivers and objectives, but the success of the organisation is the key. CEOs want HR to be orchestrators of the business strategy, not simply executing HR processes without any thought for the context. Like leaders in most fields, they expect HR to be contextually grounded.*

This requires HR leaders to demonstrate a level of commerciality and to understand the critical drivers of organisational success.

For as long as I can remember, this has been discussed as a critical capability for Human Resources professionals and, unfortunately, one that has been sadly lacking.

When I was at the National Australia Bank (NAB), we were implementing the new people and culture operating model. This was way back in 2000/2001. A whole program of work was put in place to support the implementation of the new HR system (SAP); align the HR organisation with what is now best described as the 'Dave Ulrich' model of HR delivery (business partners, shared services, centres of excellence and HR leadership); and equip the workforce with the right skills and competencies to succeed in this new model. Perhaps unsurprisingly, commercial acumen was identified as a key capability gap for the Human Resources workforce at NAB, along with consulting skills.

Twenty years later, commercial or business acumen is still, in my view, a critical skill gap for HR professionals. Arguably, consulting skills are also still somewhat lacking. In August 2019, Dave Ulrich was interviewed by David Green of myHRfuture. He maintains that 'the most important thing that HR can give an employee is a company that wins in the marketplace'. He went on to add that 'it's not just about the skills you've got, it's how those skills will drive outcomes that make a difference in what matters'. HR leaders who understand the business and proactively contribute to solving business challenges are critical for the company to win in the marketplace.

So, what does 'being commercial' really mean? Some examples of questions you should be able to articulate answers to are:

- What business is your company in?
- What is the product and/or service the company sells?
- Is it a customer, product or sales-led organisation? Or something else?

- How do the financials work?
- What is the company worth? If listed, where does it fall in the ASX listing in terms of market capitalisation?
- What is the value chain or operating model of the organisation? That is, how is the product or service produced and delivered to the customer?

Take five minutes to see how well you can currently answer those questions. Where are your strengths and weaknesses?

Personally, I am not particularly good at retaining some of the key financial metrics. It is just not my forte. If I were brilliant at numbers, I would have gone into finance or accounting. However, I do know where to find them. I make a commitment to myself to get close to the CFO whenever I begin work with a new organisation; hopefully, they become one of my closest allies. I am fortunate to have worked with some amazing CFOs, some of whom remain friends with me today.

It is critical that finance and HR are closely aligned. After all, labour (your workforce) is usually the single biggest company cost.

Although reeling off the answers to the above questions won't suddenly make you a commercial genius, you will find it helps you to have informed discussions with your CEO and peers. It will also assist you in formulating a more focused and relevant people strategy.

As the HR leader, it will show those around you
that you have an interest in the company you work
for and genuinely care about business outcomes.

It is essential that you play an active role within the executive team, contributing to the overall strategy and determining the organisational goals – and not just in terms of people, but also customers, financials, products, critical organisational projects, and risk and governance matters. You commit to the strategy and the company-wide plan to deliver on it.

ADDING VALUE

So, why is demonstrating a commitment to your business so important for you? You probably feel you have enough on your plate without trying to understand all the financials and other aspects of the company operations. I am sure, like most HR leaders, you would also say you are very commercial and of course you are committed to the business.

I remember doing some interview preparation with my good friend Deb, who worked in the executive search space. I had recently left the NAB after fifteen years and needed some help finding a new role. She asked me what differentiated me from everyone else. It was a good question. Of course, I said that I was commercial and business focused. She said that everyone says that – I needed to be able to articulate what that meant and why I was different. This was easier said than done. It took quite a lot of questioning to elicit a reasonable and accurate response. As I continued to speak about my experience, it became very clear to Deb that the way I answered her questions was different; it was all about the business and I used very little HR jargon, if any. This was apparently quite unique for an HR leader and something I have learnt to leverage. It has proven critical to my personal and professional credibility with senior stakeholders.

I mentioned earlier the constant refrain of many HR professionals: 'How do I get a seat at the table?' I've found myself reflecting that if you have to ask this question, then you are sort of missing the point altogether.

Perhaps the question should be:

'What am I doing or not doing that is impacting my ability to get cut-through with the CEO or senior executive team?'

In these same conversations, I rarely hear any reference to the actual business the HR professional is in, the organisational problems they are trying to solve or the critical factors for their organisation's success (including people).

I'm sure, if you are reading this, you have heard the same refrain many times. You've possibly even stopped attending many HR events or conferences because of this very fact. But are you also guilty of the same thinking?

*In your conversations, are you talking about the
business and the business problems you are solving?*

Building personal credibility must start with some level of
self-awareness. Being honest with yourself about your commitment to the business, your understanding of how the business
operates and your willingness to delve into the commercial drivers
of the organisation's success is the first step.

In research conducted by McKinsey and Company, CEOs, company directors and presidents were asked: 'Do you believe that
HR could be a high-impact business partner?' Eighty per cent of
those interviewed said it was critical or very important that HR
be in that role. However, only twelve per cent believed they were
actually playing that role within their organisation. In addition,
Nick Holley's research found that only thirty-seven per cent of
the CEOs and senior leaders they interviewed thought their HR
leaders knew their business well enough. A significant proportion
of those interviewed believed their heads of HR were preoccupied
with a narrow HR agenda.

This research brings home the points I've been stressing. As an
HR leader, you need to have impact. To build credibility as an
HR leader, you need to understand your business. Good CEOs
view their HR leaders as critical members of the executive team;
this means taking accountability for business performance and
delivery of the strategy.

BUILDING CREDIBILITY THROUGH COMMITMENT

There are several practical steps you can take to build your credibility with your CEO. Few of these have anything to do with your technical competence. This is a given and to be expected. At this level, the CEO expects that HR is across the basics and these will just 'get done'. What they want and need is an HR leader who cares as much about the business as they do.

There are six critical qualities I believe an HR leader needs to understand and build upon to demonstrate commitment to the business. The '6Cs' are courage, curiosity, collaboration, confidence, communication and consistency, as shown in Figure 3.1.

Figure 3.1: The 6Cs

Courage	• What actions have you taken recently that demonstrates the strength of your convictions and a certain level of bravery?
Curiosity	• Think about a time when you sought to understand something outside your area of expertise. • Do you demonstrate a strong desire to learn how your business operates and what they key drivers of success are in your organisation?
Collaboration	• How do you work with others across your business to achieve the best outcome for the business?
Confidence	• Do you appreciate your own abilities and qualities and how they can be brought to bear on the broader business strategy?
Communication	• Do you role-model great business leadership by showing vulnerability when appropriate, being transparent in your communications, and sharing your knowledge and ideas in order to influence business outcomes for success?
Consistency	• Do you demonstrate consistent behaviours and values when solving problems and business challenges? • Would your manager, peers and team describe you as consistent in the way in which you operate?

Take some time to reflect on the questions in Figure 3.1.

The 6Cs can play out in many ways and you don't need to be applying all of them all of the time. But let's look at some examples of how you can utilise the 6Cs as you seek to grow your credibility through building better relationships with and securing respect from your CEO, your executive colleagues and your team.

Courage

In executive team meetings, be passionate and open, reserve judgement where possible, demonstrate empathy, challenge where appropriate (be courageous) and say what you think. Contribute! You are not there only as the HR leader; you are there to contribute to the whole discussion as an equal member of the team.

A slightly different approach is required for the board. Your chairperson is key. If this is your first role where you need to report to a board or you are new to a company, then request time with the chair of the board and the chair of the remuneration or people committee. It is essential that you have a clear understanding of their priorities, what they want to see from you and the reporting required. Obviously, your CEO will provide some insight, but don't just take their views; they have one perspective only. Be brave, take the initiative and seek some time with them. The more they understand you and how you work – and you them – the smoother the board meetings should be. This can take huge pressure off you and provide your CEO with some breathing space and confidence that you have things in hand.

CEOs want more than passive support from their HR leader; they want unbiased views. They expect to be challenged on people issues and their leadership style.

Collaboration

Build strong relationships with your CEO, the executive team (your peers) and the board. Make regular times to meet with your peers. You are there to help and support them, and these meetings also provide great intel on key business and people issues. Don't go with your task list; use your consulting skills.

Listen, ask questions and seek clarity if you don't understand. Steven Covey talks about this exact point in his fifth habit from *The 7 Habits of Highly Effective People*. According to Covey, people usually listen with the intent to reply, not understand. Empathetic listening plays a major role in effective communication. It helps you to see things from the other person's perspective, providing a deeper insight into what is really going on. Be curious and take a genuine interest in them as people and as the leaders of their business areas. If you have tasks that require their input, call this out at the start and make sure enough time is left to get these resolved. Your needs are just as important as theirs.

Use this time to discuss how you might collaborate with them to support their business outcomes.

Confidence

To truly build credibility, your peers and CEO need to know you are a normal human being. They need to understand you as a person. What makes you tick? Will you be the fun police? Have the confidence to be yourself around your peers and team. This demonstrates a level of authenticity and comfort with who you are and a level of self-assuredness. You need to be highly adaptable as there will be times (unfortunately) when that fun might switch over into something not so fun or something inappropriate. If you have built your credibility and your team know you understand them and the company, it is much easier to step into that HR role quickly and without fuss, and hopefully address the issue efficiently and respectfully.

The HR leadership role can be difficult; you must learn how to balance being on the team and in the team.

Curiosity

If you don't fully understand the business you are in, then during those first few months you should spend time in each of the business areas. This is hard to do in terms of a time commitment, but if you do not do this in the first few months, you are highly unlikely to find the time later on.

This comes back to some level of self-awareness. If you really do grapple with finances – the terminology and the reporting – then go and do a basic finance course or ask your CFO or Finance Director to take you through a finance 101 for your business. A basic understanding of the Profit and Loss (P&L) statement and the Balance Sheet are essential. Also, there will be different terms for different industries. In the various businesses I have worked in, some examples of different languages include: bookings and sales for software subscription businesses; debt-to-income ratios, return on capital and positive 'jaws' (the graph that represents income versus expenses) in the financial services industry; physicals (e.g. mobile handsets), propex (project operating expenditure) versus opex (operating expenditure) and capex (capital expenditure) in telcos.

If you have never worked in a role that requires interaction with a board, consider doing a course through the Australian Institute of Company Directors (AICD) or do the AICD diploma. All these things do take some time and effort, but if you are genuinely interested in your business and seek to be a credible HR leader, you must address the gaps in your business knowledge.

Learn what you do not know.

Communication

How you lead and manage your own team is going to be critical to your success. As I say to all the senior leaders I work with, you cast a long shadow. Even though you may feel no different, everyone else is watching you.

This is no different from being any other senior leader, except for one fact: You, more than any other leader, need to be seen to be role-modelling the values and behaviours expected of the whole workforce.

In addition to hiring an exceptional team to support you, you must also role-model great leadership. Not only will your team respond to this positively, leading to higher overall performance and output, but you'll be surprised how many of your colleagues observe and judge you based on how you lead your own HR team. Communication styles vary, but to build commitment and trust with your own team, I have a strong bias towards transparency and a genuine care for their wellbeing and their personal growth, supported through the sharing of knowledge and information. Building strong relationships with your own team, through effective communication and support, enables them to get on with delivering the core HR requirements to the business so you can focus on building even stronger relationships with your executive peers and the CEO.

How you behave, how you communicate, what you do and don't do and when – these are all being observed.

Consistency

Whatever your management style or leadership techniques, you must apply them consistently. Unpredictable or erratic behaviours or management techniques can cause significant distress for your team and those around you. As the HR leader in your organisation, it is important you provide as much stability as possible, particularly in work environments that are undergoing significant change or transformation. When others are erratic or responding reactively to a situation, the HR leader has a responsibility to be the anchor for the organisation.

Dr James Brown, in his blog for Seba Solutions, provides some useful advice on how to provide consistency in your leadership. He discusses the need to:

1. Define your expectations. Let people know what to expect from you and what you expect from them.

2. Establish personal rules. Let people know how you like to operate; what people should be aware of in terms of your style and preferences for ways of working.
3. Explain inconsistencies. Sometimes there is a need to deviate from your normal approach. Communicate why.

Consistency builds trust. The opposite is also true.

The 6Cs should apply equally to all your relationships across the organisation: with your CEO, your peers and your team. While I have focused heavily on building credibility with your CEO, they will expect you to be consistent in how you approach your relationships with everyone else – management and employees alike. There are many leaders (HR leaders included) who have learnt to influence those above them very successfully while demonstrating completely different behaviours to everyone else. It might take a while for your CEO to realise this, but they will in time, and this approach will do little to build trust, respect or credibility with them.

BUILDING RESPECT AND BETTER RELATIONSHIPS

We know that credibility is critical in HR, possibly more so than in other professions. I think this is because HR is often seen to be quite reactive and, as discussed, not particularly commercial. Demonstrating an interest in the business in which you work is one thing, but truly understanding the business you are in takes genuine curiosity, commitment and desire.

CEOs and executives want and need their HR executive to be adding real value. The more you invest in understanding the underlying drivers of your business and the key issues your CEO is facing, both personally and as a leader of your organisation, the more they will listen to you and start to take your advice. You won't need to complain about 'not having a seat at the table'; you will already be there.

This can be hugely rewarding for you personally. You will be respected by your CEO and peers, which provides more leeway to influence the overall business and people strategy and agenda. You will feel like you are really adding value, both to them as individuals and to the business.

We also know that as your confidence builds and people listen and take heed of your contribution, your confidence builds further. Success breeds success. I have talked about my experience at Aconex. My time there was the time when I felt most confident in my own knowledge and experience and the value I could bring to the table. The CEO and my peers would listen to what I had to say; we did not always agree, but I felt comfortable and confident in putting my position forward. I felt lucky to work in a culture where everyone's views were truly valued. We all know that this is not always the case. I also know that it may not have worked out this way if I hadn't taken a genuine interest in the strategy of the organisation and the personal growth and development of my CEO and my peers. I truly cared (and still do) about enabling them to be the best leaders they could be.

Building strong, respectful relationships with the executive team led to some fun times and friendships that have endured well beyond my time at Aconex. This is rare and something I hold onto dearly. During my time there, these relationships and friendships provided a genuine outlet and opportunity to share when things got tough. There will always be difficult and stressful periods during your executive career and things can and will go wrong. Building credibility and having the respect of your peers and the people around you provides a valuable foundation that will help you when this occurs. They won't work against you; they will rally around to support you.

In my experience, the feeling of adding significant value to those around you and to the organisation and workforce you are enabling is truly rewarding.

Demonstrating a genuine commitment to the business through courage, curiosity, collaboration, confidence, communication and consistency is critical to building your credibility as an HR leader.

Exercise: How well do you know your company?

Answer the following questions without looking up the company intranet or annual report.

If you don't know the answers, do you know where you could find them?

Pull this information together into a single page to refer to when needed!

1. What is the company purpose?
2. What are the company values?
3. What are the key business drivers for your company?
4. What is the company strategy and the timeframe for delivery?
5. Is your business a product-led, customer-led or sales-led organisation?
6. What are the overarching company goals?
7. How does your company deliver to its customers (i.e. what is the company value chain or operating model)?
8. What is the single biggest challenge your company needs to solve to be successful?
9. What is the market capitalisation or annual turnover of your company?

IDENTIFY OPPORTUNITIES FOR LEARNING

I was having a chat recently with one of our young and ambitious new HR consultants. We met in person as she wanted to share her wonderful news that she was pregnant with her first child. We got onto discussing the need for additional or further studies, which she was considering undertaking while on parental leave. I thought this was somewhat ambitious based on my own experience, but that's not the point here! She had been discussing with her friend whether an MBA was worth doing. Her friend had felt that employers didn't really put much weight on these degrees any more, that this was something everyone did nowadays and it wouldn't really differentiate someone from the pack. I was a little surprised by this assessment. It seemed they were only viewing further education through one lens – seeing this type of further study as useful only in so far as it could help them achieve career advancement.

There are other very good reasons to consider doing an MBA. The MBA I undertook was considered traditional. It was heavily focused on finance, accounting, marketing and international business. I had either not learnt any of these subjects in my undergraduate degree or they were skimmed over superficially. I did my MBA for two reasons:

1. I felt I had a significant skills gap in these areas. If I were to truly progress my career in HR, I needed to understand basic and advanced business concepts.
2. I knew this would demonstrate my ability to learn, manage time effectively, prioritise tasks and apply myself.

The latter reason could apply to any study course.

As an HR leader, I strongly encourage you to pursue further study, courses or reading that enhance your business skills over and above your technical HR expertise. This will not only demonstrate your commitment, but assist you to have the right conversations, build strong relationships with your CEO and peers, and earn the respect you deserve as you confidently contribute to the strategy and performance of your business.

Chapter 4

Deliver with Integrity

EARLY IN MY CAREER I REPORTED TO A VERY SENIOR HR LEADER who was made redundant, and the memory of that has forever stayed with me.

This HR leader had only been in their role for two years and, like most HR leadership roles, it was challenging and difficult. The company in question was a complex organisation with a culture of bureaucracy, individualism and functional silos. My understanding was that it wasn't the leader's choice to leave and, unusually, she didn't see the decision coming. In HR you are often the orchestrator of your own exit, and if not the orchestrator, at least very aware of the imminent outcome.

I suspect it was the first time in her career that this leader hadn't seen the redundancy coming, wasn't expecting it and had no control over the process. It was later clear to all of us in the team what had happened, except, unfortunately, the HR leader herself. It was horrible to watch it play out for her. However, what was most distressing was observing the actions, attitude and behaviours of a member of her team who was one of my peers. I was shocked and surprised that someone, especially someone in HR, could behave in this way.

This team member was bright, outgoing and fun, and worked extraordinarily hard. He was a very talented member of the HR team and had earned great respect from his peers and business colleagues. He was also ambitious. But ambition is not a dirty word and the team and the HR leader supported his desire to succeed and progress.

Following a change of CEO, the focus of the business shifted from growth and the customer to removing costs – and quickly. It was widely believed that the HR leader who was made redundant represented one of those costs. The timing of her redundancy also seemed logical. It followed the departure of the senior business leader she worked for and with, and this was not uncommon in the world of HR. What was a little unusual, however, was the immediate promotion and appointment of another business leader into the executive role and our ambitious team member's immediate promotion into the HR leader role supporting the business leader – the role that had supposedly been made redundant. This all happened very quickly, with no obvious processes to ensure the right people were being promoted.

Perhaps naïvely, I never thought much of this at the time; it did seem that the team member was the logical successor to the now departed HR leader. However, what all of us did see eventually, and what many in the team knew all along, was that this wasn't a natural and logical appointment. In fact it became very apparent to everyone in the team, except the HR leader who was made redundant, that she had been actively undermined in the pursuit of personal ambition and promotion.

We will never know for sure, but the signs were there that the leader's redundancy and team member's subsequent promotion had been orchestrated by the senior business leader who was also promoted. It became evident that both had publicly and privately sowed the seeds of concern regarding the HR leader's capability and her alignment with the new strategy and focus of the organisation. This all sounds like something out of a conspiracy manual; however, those close to the people involved witnessed this first-hand.

As I progressed in my career, these events caused me to reflect on my own behaviour and perhaps my political naivety. What could I have done differently? Was I complicit in this outcome due to my own inaction or willingness to raise something with key decision makers? Unfortunately, these events are not uncommon and they permanently affected my view of the HR team member's integrity – both as a person and as an HR leader.

As a senior Human Resources leader, it is not only necessary but expected that integrity is core to who you are.

TRUST AND INTEGRITY

The story above is, unfortunately, not uncommon.

Many HR leaders today do not act with integrity. It is a core characteristic that is often sadly lacking.

It still amazes me, and I have been working in this field for a very long time now, how many individuals in the Human Resources field and adjacent professions of organisational development or culture do not demonstrate the values essential for someone in the profession of enabling people and engaging the workforce. It is like the plumber who doesn't fix their own leaking taps at home. Many very senior HR leaders I have come across, and worked with or for, do not seem to care too much about people. They demonstrate little empathy towards others, tend not to live the values of the organisations they represent, and care a lot more about how they are perceived. In some cases, they seem to be actively working against the organisation they work for.

This is, of course, a massive generalisation, and you could argue this is true of many senior executives or leaders. Unfortunately, you would be right – except there is one distinguishing factor. Human Resources is supposed to be about people! Humans!

So, what is integrity? *The Macquarie Dictionary* defines integrity as: 'soundness of moral principle and character; uprightness; honesty'.

Building trust through honesty, transparency and role-modelling of values is essential to delivering with integrity.

Trustworthiness and integrity are two of the most critical elements to becoming a credible HR leader; this was illustrated in Figure 2.2 in Chapter 2. For this reason, I would like to focus on how the building of trust is inextricably linked to integrity and why this is so important for you to be successful as a senior HR leader.

David Maister, Charles Green and Robert Galford authored the excellent book *The Trusted Advisor*. I strongly recommend you take the time to read it. In it, the authors introduce the concept of the Trust Equation. It is obviously not a scientific equation, but a useful frame of reference and essential reading for HR leaders.

The Trust Equation

$$\text{Trustworthiness} = \frac{\text{Credibility} + \text{Reliability} + \text{Intimacy}}{\text{Self-Orientation}}$$

Credibility in this context is your HR expertise, your technical know-how AND your understanding of and commitment to the business, embodied in the critical qualities discussed in the 5Cs model in the last chapter.

Reliability is about whether your CEO, your peers and your team think you are dependable and can be trusted to behave in consistent ways. This links your intentions with action. As an HR leader, this is about doing what you say you are going to do.

Intimacy is needed to make a connection. Getting to know the people you work with at a deeper level, and allowing them to get to know you. All too often, we hold ourselves back from exposing things of a personal nature. Doing so makes us feel vulnerable and can seem risky. As an HR leader, your ability to understand your CEO – what motivates them, what they enjoy, and elements of their personal life they are willing to share – deepens the emotional connection. It enables you to broach subjects that are important to their success and business performance that you otherwise may have avoided. It enables you to approach business-critical issues with candour.

Mastering the top line of this equation will have a significant positive impact on whether you are perceived as trustworthy by your CEO and colleagues. These elements are critical to your ability to deliver with integrity and honesty.

Self-Orientation, conversely, is a powerful dis-abler. It means focusing on yourself and demonstrating little care for others. As the equation illustrates – the higher your self-orientation, the lower your perceived trustworthiness. You will not be in a position to deliver with integrity.

The story at the beginning of this chapter illustrates the significant negative impact self-orientation can have on a senior HR leader's overall credibility. The team who worked for the HR leader's successor, his peers and other critical stakeholders all thought that he was a great HR professional but not an HR leader they could trust. Imagine people thinking about you in this way!

Trust and integrity go together. They enable you to move into a trusted advisor role, becoming a confidant for the CEO and other senior stakeholders. This is something many HR leaders aspire to achieve and it is a privilege that can be consciously worked towards.

HR AS CONFIDANT

According to Nick Holley's research, CEOs expect their HR leaders to be role models, upholding the values of the organisation and the behaviours expected of the rest of the workforce. They were asked the question: 'If you sacked an HR Director, what drove the decision?' The consistent answer was a failure of integrity.

A failure of integrity is a failure that cannot be tolerated.

CEOs expect their most senior people person to role-model the company values. They expect all their executives to do the same; however, there is a greater expectation on the senior HR leader as they are seen as the custodian of the company's people practices. CEOs also expect you to hold strong personal values and to call out bad behaviours.

It may sound like I am expecting you to be the epitome of good behaviour and you are probably thinking this is completely unrealistic. We might be in HR, but we are still human. We still have wants, needs, fears and aspirations, just like everyone else. This is true. No argument from me.

However, to be a successful HR leader, you must have a good grasp of what integrity means for you and, more importantly, what it means for the people you work with and for. As we have already discussed, the perception of your trustworthiness and integrity is critical to your ability to be an HR leader with impact. Without integrity, you will find it difficult to move beyond problem solving and advisory work based on your technical expertise and know-how and into more senior roles.

Delivering with integrity is important because many CEOs look for advice and support with the personal ups and downs of leadership – not just advice and support with people and organisational issues. Not all CEOs are receptive to or want this support, but many do, and once they have it they will never go back!

It is unlikely that your CEO or business leader will share anything of importance with you if they have doubts about your ability to hold that information close.

In my role as Chief People Officer at Aconex, I worked closely with the CEO, who was one of the founders, and the rest of the executive team, including the other co-founder. The two co-founders were best friends, but also in the awkward position of having a reporting relationship. This relationship was put in place before I joined the company. In my role, I worked with the CEO on his leadership style and was his informal sounding board. I would offer practical feedback, often with quite ruthless candour. He would not always agree, but was always open to this feedback and to learning. Sometimes, he just needed a reality check. Some of my advice and support was geared to how he navigated the sometimes difficult dual role he played with his co-founder, friend and, as it happened, direct report.

I did the same for the co-founder and other members of the executive team. There is no way I could have done this well if anyone felt I did not deliver with integrity. I felt extremely privileged to work with this team. They were willing to share their personal anxieties, desires and frustrations, both to progress their own learning and for the good of the whole team and, thus, the organisation. If they thought for one minute I was more interested in myself or was actively undermining any of them or breaching confidences (particularly with the co-founders) – that is, if my self-orientation were too high – there was no way they would have shared what they did. This would have significantly reduced my effectiveness as an HR leader, and would also have negatively impacted overall business performance.

If our role as the HR leader is to drive business performance, then team effectiveness and leadership are essential. Delivering with integrity is critical to your ability to influence these outcomes. There are some important behaviours to keep in mind and put into practice that will assist you in building strong relationships based on trust, which we'll turn to next.

HR AS LEADER

Delivering with integrity requires you to make some conscious decisions regarding how you will behave, what values you personally hold and whether, in fact, you want to become a confidant and trusted advisor. If you do, and I would argue you should, then there are some key behaviours you need to role-model and maintain.

A great quote from Judy Enns, from a story for *Global Business News*, speaks to this. She claims what CEOs want from HR leaders are:

'The brains of Einstein, the charisma of Kennedy, the negotiating skills of Kissinger, the marketing skills of Iacocca, the hide of a rhinoceros, the soul of Mother Theresa and the stamina of Jackie Joyner-Kersee!'

I have no doubt this is how a lot of you feel and, at times, reaching these heights may seem impossible.

It is not impossible, but it does take some thought and action. Good leaders, no matter what the discipline, have some similar attributes. Senior leaders cast long shadows. And, as I have mentioned before, the way HR leaders show up and the behaviours you display are even more on show as the custodian of good people practices and the employee experience.

To deliver with integrity, building trust is essential. To do this, you must follow six guiding rules.

1. Maintain confidentiality and be discreet

This is not negotiable. At times, you will be privy to extremely sensitive information about people, both personal and professional. Your role often requires you to maintain the strictest confidentiality.

Even where it does not, be careful and prudent with the information you hold. Be sensitive to how this information may impact others. Be thoughtful and diplomatic when dealing with sensitive information.

2. Do not play politics

I have recently been interviewing HR professionals for consultancy roles with my new business. One of the questions is: 'Tell me about a time when you were under immense stress.' In more than ninety per cent of the interviews, politics has been the underlying cause of stress.

You cannot ignore politics; they are a factor of human behaviour and your organisation is a microcosm of society. You need to be alert to what is going on in your workplace and who the key stakeholders are, and what their personal drivers are and how you will work with them. Do not be naïve to the politics, but do not actively contribute to or exacerbate the politics and definitely do not initiate them.

This takes courage and can be extremely difficult. Often, we feel we need to take a side or share information (read 'gossip') to build rapport with key stakeholders, or those we perceive to hold power or influence. We just want to be one of the team, one of the 'in' crowd, and to feel included. But gossip is not something you should be participating in. Gossip undermines your credibility.

3. Be empathetic

In the Trust Equation, caring more for yourself than others is self-orientation. Often, this self-orientation is driven by fear or lack of self-confidence. A fear of not being included, a fear of failure, a fear of not reaching our ambitions or achieving our aspirations. Fear often leads to taking less risk personally or professionally. It can lead to us competing with others and actively undermining others, including our CEO. It means we are much more focused on ourselves rather than the person or people we are with.

Do not interpret self-orientation to mean ambition or self-care. Ambition, drive, focus on success and achievement are important attributes of successful people. However, in this context, self-orientation means putting your needs before others.

When you are overly oriented to self, it can lead to being self-conscious and self-absorbed. The extent to which you are focusing on yourself and your own needs and not focusing on the person in front of you is the extent to which you won't be trusted.

In contrast, practise empathy. When you are truly focusing on the other person, you will be able to engage, listen, frame the issue, think about alternatives and commit to action.

4. Be consistent
This has been touched on earlier, but is critical to building trust. Think about how you treat your team and how you treat your peers and manager. What is your people orientation? Be the leader you expect your business leaders to be. You cannot have integrity if you say one thing to everyone else and do the opposite with your own team or colleagues.

5. Prepare to be vulnerable
Great leaders show their vulnerability. Ask for help if you need it, be transparent about things you do not understand, take calculated risks and challenge where appropriate. Remember, you have a wealth of experience. You are the expert in your field. Take a no-surprises approach to what you share with your CEO and/or peers.

6. Take risks

What is stopping you? Is it the underlying fears you have? The fear of not having the right answer, the fear of appearing stupid, the fear of not knowing where to start or the fear of being inaccurate? As David Maister et al say in *The Trusted Advisor*, 'A natural response to fear is to limit risk taking – which, in turn, limits the opportunity for trust.'

Delivering with integrity requires conscious thought and action. Building trust is key. Recognising that self-orientation driven from fear detracts from your ability to build trust is an important area of professional development for any HR leader.

Understanding your fears and learning to address them will enable you to be an HR leader with incredible impact.

LOYALTY AND RESPECT

Delivering with integrity enables you to build trust and gain loyalty. By focusing on intimacy and self-orientation in particular, you will significantly increase the perception of trustworthiness with your CEO, fellow executives and team. I haven't focused a lot on your own team in this chapter, but all of the content equally applies to them, not only in how they perceive you as a leader, but in what they themselves learn to be an important component of HR leadership.

When you lead with integrity, your CEO and peers will seek you out for your opinions and insights, not just on HR matters but on many aspects of running the business or company.

You may not like everything your CEO does, and even the best CEOs have development needs, but if you can be courageous and put your own fears and vulnerabilities to one side, you will take the right risks. You will challenge them when appropriate and you will open your eyes to what they need, not what you need. They will involve you in key decisions, they will ask your advice, they will confide in you. You will feel included and a valued member of the executive team.

You will generate loyalty from others and feel included and treated as a whole person. This is reciprocal.

Personally, I derive great value and a sense of self-worth when people feel confident enough in me to share their deepest concerns, worries and aspects of their personal lives. They show a vulnerability that may not be shared so freely with others in the workplace. It is an enormous honour and enables me to do my job well.

It is somewhat liberating to get to a place in your career and life where you feel confident in what you can bring, a place where you can be yourself and be less afraid of the consequences.

Of course, none of this is easy. Large corporates, in particular, thrive on politics and personal success to the detriment of others, and often reward the wrong behaviours in pursuit of financial gain. It is hard to be the odd one out in entrenched cultures of individualism and silo-ism. I have certainly experienced this myself and it can have a severe impact on your confidence. In your role, you have an opportunity to rise above this and even drive the change the organisation needs.

Delivering with integrity requires courage, a healthy dose of self-awareness, self-belief and confidence in your own knowledge and experience.

Exercise: Building your integrity

Answer the following questions honestly.

Do not be afraid to tap into your support networks, mentors or coach to help you work through these and ultimately address any fears or gaps. They may be holding you back.

1. What are you afraid of? Write down everything – and I mean everything – personal and professional.
2. Are these fears holding you back?
3. Are these fears stopping you from doing what you know needs to be said or done?
4. What behaviours are these fears driving in the workplace?
5. Go through your list and, keeping in mind everything you have learnt – your experience, expertise, knowledge and feedback – determine whether these fears seem rational.
6. Start to think through how you might overcome some of these fears in order to take the right risks to build trust with your CEO and your organisation.

THRIVING THROUGH ADVERSITY

In my consulting work, I have the extraordinary honour of working with some exceptionally smart and successful people. A very wise and caring executive and team coach once said to me that, often, successful people have survived some kind of trauma or navigated significant adversity in their lives. My work with founders has proved this time and again.

I had the honour of discovering this with one of my clients, a very successful founder and entrepreneur. I was there to support him in scaling his business. He had never led large teams before; he had never worked in the corporate environment. Everything he had learnt, he had taught himself.

Part of my work was to enable him to be the best leader he could be. He wasn't just the founder; he was also the CEO of a fast-growing company with a new leadership team of competent people. This required a very different skillset.

I work on the premise that 'what got you here won't get you there'. This means supporting a leader to look back on what has worked in the past, what makes them who they are today, what habits have stood them in good stead and what habits may be holding them back.

I could not have done this work with this founder if I had not built significant trust and credibility in the work I was originally employed to do – building a capable leadership team to enable them to scale more quickly.

My integrity was of utmost importance here. If I had not built trust through delivery, reliability, empathy and courage, challenging where appropriate, it is unlikely this founder would have shared anything of significance from their past. My reputation as a credible consultant would have been destroyed.

We were able to work through some significant events in their life that had formed their view on people and on what is important and what is not, leading to some pretty ingrained habits affecting their leadership style.

Having integrity and having the trust of those you work with enables them to be vulnerable and learn more about who they are in order to be better leaders. On the outside, no one will ever know what this very successful founder has been through, but will see the benefits when this leader utilises their personal learnings from their past during further challenging times. This has already been proved during the pandemic. It was incredibly rewarding for me to know that the work we had done had helped this founder, and thus their business, during this difficult time.

Chapter 5

Take Action and Accountability

Way back in 2004, seventeen years ago, the National Australia Bank was embroiled in a significant foreign exchange trading scandal that cost the bank around $360 million and put a damaging and significant dent in its reputation. It was a stressful time for senior management and also deeply hurtful and disappointing for the 30,000-strong workforce – the ninety-nine per cent of the workers who came to work every day to do a good job, serve their customers and go home, at the end of the day, proud of what they had achieved. At the time, NAB was the largest of the big four banks in Australia. It has, unfortunately, never really recovered from this scandal. Due to the significance of the fraud, ASIC – the Australian regulator – became heavily involved and issued an enforceable undertaking relating to the culture of the bank. This led to a significant program of work within the people and culture (HR) team and projects were set up and resourced to address this undertaking.

What happened next and over the many months that ensued was an extraordinary effort to address every aspect of the culture that may have led to the trading scandal. HR embarked on a mammoth

attempt to ensure that no individual would ever do this again.
The entire performance management framework was revamped,
including the introduction of compliance and behaviour gates.
This effectively meant that you could not complete the annual
performance review (read – be eligible for a bonus or incentive)
unless you got through these first two gates. The compliance
gates were relatively straightforward and included tasks such
as ensuring your compliance training was completed and up to
date; the behaviour gates were somewhat more complex! A raft
of behaviours was developed and articulated. Your people leader
had to assess your behaviours against these criteria and, where
possible, provide examples of such. If you passed the two gates,
you then went on to the normal performance review (which was
pretty complex already). This performance approach was rolled
out across the entire organisation and every single employee was
required to participate.

Fast forward a year or two following its implementation, and the
approach had been tweaked, modified and added to in such a way
that it was now a much maligned and arguably ineffective method
of managing an individual's performance. A process designed to
remove any subjectivity had, in fact, the opposite effect. Every
employee interpreted the behavioural standards against their
own personal set of values. It actually got to a point where people
leaders were asked to rate an employee's behaviours on a five-
point grading scale.

I could spend a long time here describing the impact of this both
organisationally and at an individual employee level. However,
I think you can probably work this out. In 2017, another Royal
Commission into the Australian banking system was launched.

NAB, once again, was front and centre, and for all the wrong reasons. Culture, it seemed, was the culprit yet again.

The tendency of HR leaders to react with overly complex and over-engineered solutions is, unfortunately, all too common.

Not only this, but the solutions they develop to address a problem are often targeted at the very few employees who do something wrong, not the ninety-nine per cent of the workforce who are doing the right things, every day. HR leaders must take accountability and action to address this.

HR IS TOO COMPLEX AND REACTIVE

What the story above illustrates is HR's serial tendency to overcomplicate things. As the HR leader, you have a responsibility to be proactive about delivering HR solutions and initiatives that ensure tangible business outcomes. Peter Seeger famously said,

'Any darn fool can make something complex; it takes a genius to make something simple.'

Workforces, organisations, employment laws, corporation laws, indeed, any laws, are complex. The legal responsibilities alone are extensive for any HR leader. You need to acknowledge that you are dealing with complexity and ensure that the people you work with find whatever you produce **easy to understand** and straightforward. You must accept the complexity and, while you can't necessarily make it simpler, you should try to make it **accessible** to your workforce.

Simplicity is not easy to achieve, and people are undeniably complex.

To illustrate this, let's look at the development of policies and procedures (in response to the many laws and obligations employers must comply with). In my experience, these HR policies are often complex and lengthy, and written to address the small percentage of employees who might do the wrong thing, not the majority who do the right thing!

The consequence of this can be that the workforce doesn't understand the policies or the procedures they need to follow or, perhaps worse, they don't read them at all. In addition, by assuming people will do the wrong thing, procedures are designed to consider every possible scenario to prevent this from occurring, leading to the complexity I have discussed. They are written as rules, not guidelines, and are enforced. Often, the unintended consequence of this is that approval processes and delegations are held exceptionally high in the organisation. For example, a CEO might have to sign off domestic travel requests for their direct reports so that they don't misuse their budgets. Is this the best use of a CEO's time? What impact does this have on employee engagement and productivity? Does this demonstrate trust in their workforce?

When I worked at Telstra, this was certainly the case. I was in a very senior HR role; however, for me to deliver what was required, I needed to produce business cases, go through many layers of approvals (in HR and other functions), and beg, borrow and steal funding from whomever I could, to do what I thought was right for the business and workforce I supported. It felt like I had been given significant accountability for business outcomes, but not the corresponding responsibility or resources to deliver the right HR initiatives for the business I supported. Not only was this frustrating, but it impacted my ability to deliver the required HR programs in a timely and efficient manner. It significantly impacted my productivity and took enormous energy and attention.

The complexity of HR policies and processes can undermine trust and impact productivity.

As an HR leader, you need to take accountability for not only **what** initiatives and programs you deliver, but **how** these are delivered. You need to take accountability for ensuring that HR processes are done well, and that you are engaging with leaders and managers so they understand why these processes matter. Building unnecessary complexity into these processes does not support the leaders and managers to lead their teams in the most effective way.

As Albert Einstein said, 'Make everything as simple as possible, but not simpler.'

In addition to the significant complexity HR often introduces to business, HR is also often perceived as being reactive to constantly changing priorities rather than proactive in addressing significant strategic business issues. This may be driven by competing business demands, the CEO changing their mind (often), or the HR function itself trying to address too many problems with too many new initiatives or programs at once. HR leaders are all too often caught up with operational matters. In fact, most HR leaders are still spending seventy to eighty per cent of their time on operational or tactical programs of work that the CEO has little interest in and little need for. Not only this, but you can be seen to be unresponsive and slow to take action.

Focusing too much time on operational matters and building complexity into your HR solutions will also make you extremely busy. You will not have enough time in the day to get everything done and you will feel overwhelmed and frustrated that you are unable to get to that strategic work everyone wants you to focus on.

As an HR leader, you need to take accountability for making the complex simple.

This approach will enable you to free up your time, focus on the things that really matter, and take clear action to deliver useful policies, processes and initiatives that enable your workforce to get on with what it is they need to do.

HR OUTCOMES ARE CRITICAL TO BUSINESS SUCCESS

There are two very important reasons why you need to take accountability for removing complexity and being proactive in your focus on critical business priorities to deliver useful and meaningful HR solutions.

1. Your business needs you, and
2. If you don't, you will burn out.

1. Your business needs you!

Nick Holley's research confirmed what many CEOs experience – 'It's just complete chaos around the HR function, so distracted, so reactive, so overwhelmed, so they lose credibility, so people stop listening to them.'

It is disheartening to read this, but we know through our own experience that this is often true. The reality is that what the business needs is not necessarily what HR thinks it needs. As we discussed in Chapter 3, it's important to commit to the business.

The HR leader needs to take accountability for understanding the key business priorities in order to take the right action at the right time.

The foundational elements of HR delivery are a given; these are only important or noticed by employees, senior leaders or the CEO when something goes wrong. We often talk about 'getting the basics right'. You can debate what the basics are, but this could include important actions such as paying people correctly, getting their leave right and being clear about what is expected of them. It will also most likely include some of your core HR processes, from recruitment through to exiting employees; that is, processes related to the employee lifecycle. These are not really basic at all; these are, in fact, very complex processes, but they are core to HR and it should be a given that these just work. If they don't, your job in implementing anything more strategic than this will be severely hampered, because people just won't listen.

'Good' CEOs want you to be strategic.

I have no doubt you have heard this many times and you are probably sick of hearing it and saying it yourself!

I say 'good' CEOs because there are many who are way too into the detail themselves; they constantly shift their priorities, they delve deeply into operational matters and they are often influenced by the board and/or mentors and business colleagues outside your organisation. They will often have a view on what HR should be doing based on their previous experiences and these external inputs. This is undoubtedly difficult for you to manage. If this is your experience, I can guarantee your colleagues in the executive team will also be experiencing this. This is a leadership issue, which you can influence – if you have the time!

Which brings me to point number two.

2. You will burn out!

I have touched on this previously. As the HR leader, there is a higher expectation on you to uphold the values of the organisation and be the eyes and ears of the workforce for your CEO and executive colleagues. The weight of these expectations, in addition to the relentless nature of your role, means you always feel reactive, you feel constantly overwhelmed and stressed, and there is no time to get to the strategic work which you desperately know needs to be done.

When your ability to take action and deliver the right HR outcomes for your business is compromised, it can lead to real feelings of inadequacy and impact your mental health and confidence.

Unfortunately, I have seen this all too often: relentless pressure to perform and deliver, often with little thanks or acknowledgement, leading to real impacts on work/life balance and physical and mental health. No one should feel like this because of their work.

This is about taking the right actions for your business. How you achieve this is integral to your own wellbeing and to the perception of the HR function. As the HR leader, you need to take accountability for the quality and relevance of the HR processes and solutions you have implemented.

TAKING A PRAGMATIC APPROACH TO HR

There are four critical elements to taking back some control and shifting your focus to those HR solutions that will move the business forward. By taking accountability for your current situation and taking the right action, you will increase your personal job satisfaction and improve the perception of your HR function.

These four actions are listed in Figure 5.1, along with some reflective questions to prompt your thinking.

Figure 5.1: The four critical elements

Get the basics right	• Do you have the core HR foundations in place? Do they work? If not, why not? • What action, resourcing, funding is needed to get this done?
Get a great team	• Do you have the right team in place to support you to take action? If not, why not? • What action, thinking, support and funding is required to get this done?
Get real	• Do you feel you always have to be on top of the latest HR thinking? • Do you implement solutions because you think they should be done or because you know the business strategy requires them? • What action needs to be taken to reduce the number of HR initiatives to ensure those being delivered meet a real business need?
Get going	• Have you overcomplicated the solutions? • Are you being pragmatic and commercial about what can be achieved and in what timeframe? • What action, workforce engagement and approach have been considered to deliver critical HR solutions?

Reflecting on some of these questions will enable you to start thinking about where you should be focusing your attention. I explain these actions in more detail below.

1. Get the basics right

If management and employees cannot access the tools and resources they need to do their jobs, you and your team will be constantly inundated with calls, requests and complaints.

As the HR leader, encourage your team to err towards simplicity over complexity. For example, if the majority of your workforce don't see value in your current approach to performance reviews, and they primarily see them as a compliance exercise, then seriously consider removing them altogether and then, over time, work out what is actually needed.

In larger organisations, if the basics are broken, it will be very difficult to get traction on that new leadership initiative that might be the number one thing the organisation needs – unfortunately, no one will be listening. In a smaller organisation or scale-up, you will probably have to do both at the same time – but consider what is mission critical; what is your minimum viable product? Only do what is absolutely necessary to ensure you don't over-burden the business or yourself!

If the most fundamental HR processes needed by your employees are not met, it will be almost impossible to build credibility.

2. Get a great team

I know this sounds like common sense and it should be the advice you are providing to your business, however, time and again, I see HR leaders putting this way down their priority list.

You need a combination of thinkers and doers. If you are in a small organisation, preferably try to find these traits in the one person. Make sure the team comprises the right skillsets to deliver on the most important people problem in your business. In my role at

Aconex, I had a team of sixteen for a global organisation of 900 people. I made a pact with myself that I would not increase this number, but ensure I had the right people for what we needed to do. Half the team were internal recruiters. This made sense as we needed to hire the best tech talent across the globe in a highly competitive market. The only specialist role I hired was my General Manager of Organisational Development. Through periods of rapid growth, there had been little investment in leadership capability or employee development, and it was critical to the organisation's growth strategy.

There has been much written on how the HR organisation should be structured, and what the critical capabilities are for HR now and into the future. Future trends certainly need to be taken into account; however, the most critical attribute of any team is that they are capable of doing what you need them to be doing. It also helps tremendously if you have one or two in the team who can step up and into your role occasionally.

If you do not have a team (and for start-ups and scale-ups, this is common), think about what capabilities you need to be successful. You may need to think creatively about how you get the work done. A start-up will not necessarily have the money or willingness to invest in more HR resourcing, but you may be able to bring in the right talent on short-term secondments to get critical HR processes into place.

By critically reviewing the capability of your team and what skills you need to deliver key business outcomes, you are putting your needs on a footing equal to the rest of your peers. All too often, I see HR leaders put their own resourcing needs last. This will not do you or the business you work with any good.

Your CEO wants and needs you to be successful. You will not always get all the resourcing you require, but you must be prepared to ask for it. The calibre of your team is critical to building the capability of the organisation and delivering on the overall strategy.

You must choose the best people you can afford, who complement your skills and who will support you to take action.

3. Get real

Get real about what is required and whether employees, management or senior executives will feel your efforts add value to them as individuals and to the organisation.

Before implementing that latest HR fad you read about or heard about at your last HR conference, please consider whether it is the right thing for your organisation. If it is the right thing, then is it the right timing?

I have, at times, seen HR leaders feel that to be successful and respected, they must be armed with all the latest thinking. They produce amazingly detailed and complex PowerPoint decks to prove that what they are proposing is necessary. As mentioned, one of the latest crazes was to remove performance reviews. PwC received significant and positive media attention for doing exactly this – then every HR department decided they should do the same. Now, I am obviously over-stating this, but many HR leaders did go down this path. I do understand why – as we've discussed, in general, most employees and managers find current performance processes cumbersome and of little value – but I do wonder how much thought was put into what was actually needed in any particular business and whether HR leaders just blindly followed the headlines.

New innovations and disruption are critical to continuous improvement and we are just starting to see some of this emerge across the HR domain. Organisations are embracing agile ways of working and the COVID-19 pandemic has forced significant changes to the way workforces engage with their employers. HR has overseen much of this change. Continuous learning is imperative. But... **please do not overload your business with multiple initiatives.**

By all means, understand what current best practice is, innovate and try new things, but consider what business need you are addressing and whether there is capacity across the organisation to implement and embrace the change.

*Take accountability for the HR solutions
and initiatives you are implementing.*

4. Get going!

How you deliver HR solutions is just as important as what you deliver. I have seen many great HR initiatives or programs fail due to fundamental gaps in the planning, design and implementation.

Often, at its simplest, the case for change has not been built adequately. The core principles of project management should be followed to increase the likelihood of a successful implementation.

This includes (early) stakeholder engagement and clear articulation of business benefits, business impact/risks, resourcing requirements (human and financial) and implementation timelines. Most importantly, involvement of employees in the design phase and throughout the entire development of the new initiative should be a given. Often, new programs are designed and implemented with little involvement from the end user until a 'testing' phase – this is way too late.

In larger organisations, there may be a programmatic approach; however, each centre of excellence (CoE) is doing the same thing – there needs to be a coordination point to ensure the different initiatives make sense as a whole, that they are integrated and that the business has the capacity to implement and embrace the change, ensuring its ongoing viability and sustainability. I have seen enormous waste, where significant money and resources have been put into projects only for them to be thrown out six months to a year later and derided as ineffective and over-engineered HR rubbish.

Involvement and engagement of employees and 'end-users' or 'internal customers' early in the design and throughout the development will ensure your solutions are pragmatic, not overly complex and relevant to those who will be using them. Utilising a project management approach including change management, capacity planning and communication requirements will increase the likelihood of a successful and sustainable implementation of your HR initiative.

A clear understanding of the business need and the benefits to your workforce will help you to prioritise and get going.

GETTING BUSINESS RESULTS

By consistently focusing on what is most important to the business and regularly reviewing your strategy, initiatives and activities, your ability to influence key stakeholders with credibility and confidence will increase. You may even feel some sense of relief.

What I am proposing is not easy. As the HR leader, you will always have competing priorities, there will always be urgent and unforeseen problems to solve and, if you are in a large company, particularly a publicly listed entity, there will be constant pressure from your CEO, peers and your own team to deliver a multitude of HR solutions, always in a very short period. The larger and more sophisticated your team, the more they will produce in their desire to add value. This is something fairly and squarely in your remit to control. You must take accountability for the business outcomes and the actions you and your team are taking to deliver them.

I am often asked how I managed to move into these very senior roles and maintain some semblance of work/life balance. I had good support at home, which certainly helped, but there were periods of immense stress and probably times when I bordered on complete burnout. I have, unfortunately, seen this many times with the HR leaders I have worked with over the years.

If this sounds a bit like you, then stop – right now. There is a better way and it doesn't need to be like this. Remember the four critical actions you must take to enable you to deliver pragmatic and useful HR solutions to organisational problems:

1. **Get the basics right** – Ensure the HR foundations are strong and employees understand the core HR policies and procedures that enable them to work productively and positively.
2. **Get a great team** – The most important action you can take. Ensure you hire HR practitioners who are pragmatic, smart and will support you.
3. **Get real** – Understand your business, engage with the workforce and understand what is truly needed. Avoid over-complicated, over-engineered HR solutions.
4. **Get going** – Utilise project management principles, engage the workforce and take action.

Taking accountability and action for the delivery of tangible, cost-effective and useful HR solutions will provide the platform for greater access to support, resourcing and recognition. Your CEO and executive peers will actively support you to deliver critical business outcomes because they will see you as proactive, with a clear plan to address issues of the most concern to them and the organisation.

Perhaps even more importantly, you provide yourself with some breathing space to spend time on what matters most, whether that be at work or at home.

Exercise: Take action – now!

Take some time and articulate the single biggest problem your organisation is trying to solve. Not the people problem – the biggest business problem.

Review your list of HR initiatives (or HR delivery roadmap) and the timeframes in which you were planning to implement these.

Reflect on the number of initiatives to be delivered, the timeframes and the intended benefits to employees and/or the organisation. Do any of these initiatives address the single biggest problem the organisation is trying to solve?

If so, excellent – but get real about all those other initiatives that don't!

If none of these HR initiatives address the biggest business problem, then go back to the drawing board. It's time to review your people strategy, areas of focus and the activities you and your team are working on.

BUT THAT'S NOT HR!

When you take the approach of solving the biggest business challenge, this can lead to confusion from both your non-HR and your HR colleagues. During my time at Telstra, the number one issue the organisation was trying to solve was customer advocacy. Under the then CEO, David Thodey, customer advocacy was the number one performance criteria. It was cascaded as a key performance indicator from the most senior leaders right through to the call centre and retail store staff and measured by the net promotor score (NPS).

I led Human Resources for the Retail division. Some 20,000 employees who directly impacted customer outcomes. Working with external consultants, I formulated a business case to develop a specialised centre for customer capability. Its purpose was to increase the internal employee capability to resolve customer problems (rather than heavily relying on external professional services firms). This was not standard HR practice! Although in my mind this was clearly linked to the organisational agenda and clearly related to the people function (that is, increasing capability) – it was not so clear to any of my colleagues! I had enormous difficulty convincing the business I supported that this was something I should be leading, and little, if any, understanding from the Human Resources leadership group that this was something our function could make a significant impact upon. Not only was I pushing the boundaries of what constituted HR, but for this to be successful I needed support from different divisions across

Telstra – this flew in the face of what continued to be very siloed behaviour across the organisation.

I persisted. I took the business feedback on board and proactively sought support from other parts of Telstra, particularly those focused on customer advocacy and experience. After many months of perseverance and a healthy dose of resilience, I succeeded in obtaining the support of the Retail Leadership Team to trial this. They funded the pilot. We used methodologies such as systems thinking and design thinking to train our employees in these methods. We brought in real customers, involving them in the solving of real customer problems. I was very proud of what we achieved; however, it was extremely difficult to get this up and running. Sometimes, you will need to be courageous and bold in pushing forward strong people solutions for business problems, especially if it doesn't seem to fit the 'normal' HR mould!

Conclusion

Putting this into Practice

A GOOD FRIEND OF MINE IS NAVIGATING THE COMPLEXITIES OF a pandemic, a merger, a potential exit event and challenging workplace politics at the most senior level. She has a solid team, but not a team with significant breadth or depth of experience. She has a young family. She is more than capable and has somehow survived a crazy year with her sense of humour intact. But this is not sustainable, and I'm concerned she will burn out soon.

I have no doubt her story resembles many of your stories. At some point, you may wonder, 'Why am I doing this?' There may have been times throughout the year when your work has started to affect your own health and wellbeing.

Leadership is stressful at the best of times, let alone with the added burden and expectations placed on you as the most senior HR leader. Not only have you had to endure and lead through one of the most challenging periods in recent history – the global COVID-19 pandemic – but you may also be enabling your organisation through significant changes unrelated to the pandemic.

The current approach to HR in many organisations has led to a crisis of confidence in the function, and the rolling of eyes whenever you mention you are from HR. It has also, unfortunately, led to over-stretched, stressed HR professionals with little resources or support to enable them to be as effective as possible. This becomes a never-ending, vicious circle and ultimately leads to some great HR leaders leaving the profession for good. People issues are complex; internal politics, difficult senior leaders with poor behaviours and poor performance from your team make them even more complex.

But change is possible and it starts with you!

I have been fortunate throughout my career to work with some exceptional CEOs, senior leaders and HR professionals. I have learnt a lot and continue to learn. At the heart of much of what I have discussed is good leadership. However, I truly believe that for HR to be effective and respected, and for you to feel like you are adding value to your organisation, there needs to be change. We should be willing to share our stories to support those who come after us. I have endeavoured to provide some insights into what I believe makes a good HR leader to support you in one of the most difficult and undervalued roles in an organisation.

Often, these things are not spoken of and we all must find our own way. But people are complex, expectations from our CEOs and peers are increasing, and there is still massive gender imbalance at the most senior levels of our businesses, which creates another layer of complexity altogether.

My hope for you in reading this book is that you understand the three practical steps you can take to become a successful and credible HR leader:

1. Commit to your business
2. Deliver with integrity
3. Take action and accountability

A commitment to the business requires HR leaders to demonstrate a high degree of commerciality and to understand the critical drivers of organisational success. As the HR leader, you should be viewed as a critical member of the executive team, taking accountability for business performance and delivering the strategy.

As the HR leader, it is not only necessary but expected that integrity is core to who you are. HR leaders must role-model, upholding the values of the organisation and the behaviours expected of the rest of the workforce. Delivering with integrity will enable you to build trust and gain loyalty.

Finally, the HR leader must take action and accountability for the services, solutions and initiatives the HR function delivers. Ensure the foundational employee processes and procedures are done well and consistently, focus on solving the biggest, most important business issues, and prioritise, prioritise, prioritise.

With a little bit of insight into what is needed to build credibility in your role as HR leader and with practice and support from your CEO, peers and external mentors, I believe we can grow a new generation of empathetic, commercial HR professionals who will go on to do great things. The pandemic has created an opportunity too good and too painful to squander.

It is time to put some of these steps into practice.

HR is too important to give up on. Together, we can and we should deliver HR with impact!

Resources

The following books and articles have informed my thinking along the way, and I am sure you will find them useful as you look to create more impact through your HR leadership.

Adams, Lucy (2017). *HR Disrupted: It's time for something different.* Practical Inspiration Publishing.

Armstrong, Martin (2020). *HR's Secret Weapon? Business Acumen.* Workforce Institute, www.workforceinstitute.org

Bersin, Josh (2020). *The World Just Changed Overnight. The New World of Work and How HR Must Respond.* Josh Bersin Academy, www.bersinacademy.com

Bersin, Josh (2020). *Responding to COVID-19. Ten Lessons from the World's HR Leaders.* Josh Bersin, www.joshbersin.com

Brown, Dr James (2016). *Consistency – A Critical Leadership Trait.* Seba Solutions Inc., www.sebasolutions.com

Holley, Nick (2014). *What CEOs want from HR.* Executive Education, Henley Business School, www.henley.ac.uk

Mackowiak, Jerome; Whittle, Mark (2020). *How Agile Principles Drive Successful HR Transformations*. Gartner Inc. www.gartner.com/en/human-resources

Maister, David; Green, Charles; Galford, Robert (2002). *The Trusted Advisor*, Simon & Schuster UK Ltd, www.simonandschuster.co.uk

Mazor, AH; Alburey, A; Volini, E; Bowden, M; Stephan, M. (2014) 'The High-Impact HR Operating Model. HR has a new mission. Here is the plan'. Deloitte Development LLC, www.deloitte.com/au/articles

Mazor, AH; Stephane, J; Baker Calamai, J; Johnsen, G; Hill, A; Moen, B. (2019) 'Exponential HR. Break away from the traditional operating models to achieve work outcomes'. Deloitte Development LLC, www.deloitte.com/au/articles

Milligan, Susan (2018). 'HR2025: 7 Critical Strategies to Prepare for the Future of HR'. SHRM magazine, www.shrm.org

Simons, Tony (2008). *The Integrity Dividend. Leading by the power of your word*. Jossey-Bass, an imprint of John Wiley & Sons.

Trammel, Joel (2016). '4 Things CEOs want from HR Leadership', www.entrepreneur.com

Trusted Advisor (Associates LLC), Blog. 'HR Leaders as Trusted Business Advisors', www.trustedadvisor.com/articles

Ulrich, D; Allen, J; Brockbank, W; Younger, J; Nyman, M (2009). *HR Transformation. Building Human Resources from the Outside In.* McGraw Hill.

Ulrich, D; Younger, J; Brockbank, W; Ulrich, M (2012). *HR from the Outside In.* McGraw Hill.

Connect with Me

IF YOU HAVE FOUND THIS BOOK USEFUL AND YOU THINK I MAY be able to support you in your quest for more impactful HR, then I would love for us to connect. They say the first book is the hardest, so as a first-time author it would be wonderful to hear your insights and feedback. What have you taken from this book? What have I missed?

In my role as CEO and co-founder of shilo., it is my business to support HR leaders to be the best they can be. We operate across Australia with ambitions to provide our brand of HR globally.

If you need exceptional HR talent to supplement or complement your team on a short to medium-term basis, then I would love to hear from you. shilo. consultants share our commitment to providing pragmatic HR solutions so that you can focus on leveraging your relationships, building credibility and influencing critical business outcomes.

My work naturally leads me to provide informal mentoring and advice to senior HR leaders, as clients, colleagues and often friends.

The best ways to get in touch are:

- ✉ ilona@shilopeople.com
- 🌐 www.shilopeople.com
- 🔗 ilonacharles
- 📷 shilo.people
- 📘 shilo.people
- 🐦 ilonacharles1

Acknowledgements

As I sit down to write these acknowledgements, I feel proud to be finally in the position to do so. To write a book, let alone my first book, takes a massive commitment and a huge team effort.

To those of you who believed I could do this and encouraged me from day one – my partner Aaron and my sons Jack and Max. Although I'm not sure they quite realised what was involved, they believed in me and my ability to get this done.

To Wendy Born, a successful author of two books, a friend and colleague who suggested I write a book in the first place. You introduced me to the right people and you were the first person to read a very early draft – thank you!

A massive thank you to Sharna Peters, co-founder of shilo., friend, business partner and one of the most caring people I know, for giving me time, listening to my venting, believing in me and providing ongoing encouragement when we were building a business. Thank you also for picking up the extra workload when I needed to meet deadlines.

A big thank you to Kelly Irving, without whose guidance, advice and focus I would not be sitting here today writing these acknowledgements. She is an editor extraordinaire. Her ability to take a jumbled mess of thoughts and content and turn it into something readers might actually understand is remarkable. Thank you also to the amazing group of fellow authors in the group coaching sessions.

To Sara, Carolyn, Scott and all the team at Grammar Factory Publishing. Your care, understanding and support through the final edits and publishing have been phenomenal. Nothing was ever too much trouble.

Thank you to the people who read early drafts of my book; you know who you are. Your feedback was super helpful, and I cannot believe you took the time to read the book right through and provide wonderfully constructive and beneficial feedback!

Finally, thank you to you. The reader. I trust you will find some pearls of wisdom and nuggets of advice in this book that support you in your quest to become a credible and respected HR leader.

About the Author

ILONA IS PASSIONATE ABOUT PEOPLE. SHE FUNDAMENTALLY believes that we come to work each day to do the best we can – no matter what role we are in, or level we are at.

As the CEO and co-founder of shilo., an Australian business dedicated to providing exceptional HR talent to organisations nationally, she supports senior HR leaders to be their best. Along with her co-founder, Ilona is intent on disrupting and challenging the HR profession to not just think but act differently. Ilona is renowned for her authentic and pragmatic approach to leadership and Human Resources.

As a Human Resources executive with over twenty-five years' experience in leadership and transformation roles, Ilona also mentors aspiring HR leaders and former colleagues who now 'find themselves' in senior HR leadership roles. She has built friendships and mentoring relationships with her clients at companies like Buildxact, CyberCX, and Atlas Arteria.

She is also a qualified Occupational Therapist, which, she believes has provided her with the core foundational skills to become an exceptional HR leader. In addition, she has a Master of Business

Administration and is a graduate of the Australian Institute of Company Directors.

Ilona lives in Melbourne with her family: a wonderful partner of ten years and two beautiful boys aged twenty-one and nineteen. While she doesn't have much spare time these days, she does like to eat good food, drink nice wine and hopes to travel again one day.

Ilona truly believes that HR as a profession can have substantially more impact. She believes that if we put the human back into HR and treat people as adults and with respect, HR leaders can make a massive difference to a lot of people – including themselves.

www.shilopeople.com

www.ingramcontent.com/pod-product-compliance
Lightning Source LLC
Chambersburg PA
CBHW030527210326
41597CB00013B/1060